Relax—
You May Only Have a Few Minutes Left

Relax—
You May Only
Have a Few
Minutes Left

Using the Power of Humor
to Overcome Stress
in Your Life and Work

LORETTA LaROCHE

HAY HOUSE, INC.
Carlsbad, California • New York City
London • Sydney • Johannesburg
Vancouver • Hong Kong • New Delhi

Published and distributed in the United States by: Hay House, Inc.: www. hayhouse.com • **Published and distributed in Australia by:** Hay House Australia Pty. Ltd.: www.hayhouse.com.au • **Published and distributed in the United Kingdom by:** Hay House UK, Ltd.: www.hayhouse.co.uk • **Published and distributed in the Republic of South Africa by:** Hay House SA (Pty), Ltd.: www. hayhouse.co.za • **Distributed in Canada by:** Raincoast: www.raincoast.com • **Published in India by:** Hay House Publishers India: www.hayhouse.co.in

Editorial supervision: Jill Kramer

First published in 1998 by Villard Books, a division of Random House, Inc.: ISBN: 0-375-50145-2.

Library of Congress Cataloging-in-Publication Data

LaRoche, Loretta.
  Relax-- you may only have a few minutes left : using the power of humor to overcome stress in your life and work / Loretta LaRoche. -- Rev. ed.
      p. cm.
  ISBN-13: 978-1-4019-1769-2 (pbk.)
  1. Stress (Psychology) 2. Stress management. 3. Wit and humor--Therapeutic use. 4. Laughter--Therapeutic use. I. Title.
  BF575.S75L276 2007
    155.9'042--dc22
2006029966

ISBN: 978-1-4019-1769-2

11 10 09 08   5 4 3 2
1st edition, February 2008
2nd edition, February 2008

Printed in the United States of America

To my mom for her love, laughter,
lasagna, and heavy nagging . . . it all worked!
To my children, Jon, Laurie, and Erik, and
their spouses for keeping me humble,
and to my 11 grandchildren
for helping me stay silly.

I love you all lots!

೦೨ ೦೨ ೦೨

CONTENTS

INTRODUCTION

Three One-Dollar Bills

Recently my husband, Bob, and I were in Florida for a long overdue vacation. Bob is a wonderful guy, but like most people, including myself, he creates a lot of the stress in his life, mostly by failing to appreciate the humor in everyday situations.

In many ways, Bob and I are very different. He's a tall, ruddy-faced WASP with a shock of white hair; I'm a small, pale-skinned Italian with auburn (at the moment) hair. But our differences extend past the physical and the cultural. Bob is organized and methodical. He does everything in a routine, from eating certain foods (turkey's a favorite for lunch), to the time he goes to bed (past nine o'clock, it's lights out). On the other hand, I love spontaneity, favor a reasonable amount of disorder, and constantly question the logic behind everything.

It was a beautiful day as we rolled along the highway to Captiva Island. The top was down on the rented convertible and I was gawking at the scenery, drifting off into pleasant relaxation. Ah, I thought, my vacation is finally under way.

However, Bob, a former military man, was totally alert, barking out local landmarks that indicated that we, as he put it, "were on course." Bob's always worried about making a wrong turn, and like almost all men, he'll never stop to ask for directions. (That's why Moses spent 40 years in the desert. If he'd had a woman with him, she would have asked the burning bush.)

As Bob headed down a curving stretch of road, he spotted a sign that sent him into perfectionist overdrive: TOLL BRIDGE, THREE MILES. THREE DOLLARS.

Urgently Bob asked if I had the money. I replied, "I don't know. Don't worry. We've got plenty of time before the toll to find it." In my mind, three miles is three years away.

"I need to know if you have three one-dollar bills."

"Why? Won't a five do?"

"No." Bob was starting to get irritated. "That'll take too much time. Just look in your purse, will you?"

Well, now we were in trouble. My purse is not just a purse. My friend Myra calls it "the abyss." My purse is a large leather object that weighs in the vicinity of 15 pounds. I have enough stuff in there to conduct electrolysis and open heart surgery at the same time. Attempts to hastily retrieve any particular item usually end in frustration. But since Bob's face was starting to turn a deeper shade of pink—a sure sign of an impending fight—I began to search through the abyss, looking for those elusive dollar bills.

"Well, do you have them?" he asked.

At that moment, my fingers touched bottom and slid around a trove of coins. "I don't have any bills, but I've got lots of change," I said happily.

Bob groaned. "I can't give them change."

"What do you mean, you can't give them change? Who cares? Money's money!"

Bob said, "You just don't give that much change at a toll. What are we going to do?"

"We're going over the bridge, unless you have a tent in the trunk. We can't stay here."

Bob now escalated the argument into a new dimension. "I can't believe you don't understand how embarrassing this is. What will they say?" he asked.

"No, I don't understand," I replied. "Who are they? There's nothing embarrassing about giving change to a toll taker. Now, if I was naked when I handed them the change, that would be embarrassing."

When Bob wants to press his case in an argument, he shifts to a hypothetical situation, just in case my feeble mind can't grasp his point. "What if it were a hundred dollars for the toll?" he said. "Would you give them the money in change?"

Now I lost it. To me, the conversation had reached a dizzying height of illogic. I knew I made perfect sense; after all, I always do. I tried to stifle my growing anger, calling upon some of the stress-management techniques I've learned and taught over the years. I tried to elicit the "relaxation response," but it was no go. I sought my "compassionate witness," but she wasn't home. At this point, two rolls of masking tape were needed to stop my response: "There's no toll in the world that requires a hundred dollars. They don't charge a hundred dollars to get to Captiva Island. Or Gilligan's Island! Or even Treasure Island!"

Bob burst out angrily, "You're not taking this seriously. You never take me seriously."

Little did Bob know how seriously I was taking him. I was silently dipping into my storehouse of verbal nuclear weapons. My arsenal contains various forms of sarcasm, ranging from mild mockery to outright ridicule. I was reaching for the right weapon that would get Bob on his knees, praying that I would stop moving my lips.

As we neared the toll booth, I spotted the toll taker. She was a pleasant-looking blonde in her 30s who scarcely expected the Ralph and Alice Kramden exchange that was about to unfold. Bob pulled the car up to the toll booth and said loudly, "Give me the damn change."

As I handed it to him, I looked at the toll taker and asked in my sweetest voice, "Excuse me, miss, does it bother you if we give you change? And more important, if it does, will you tell anyone?"

The toll taker laughed and said, "No problem. I get change all the time." With that, Bob's face contorted, and he gripped the wheel and peeled out. Our vacation was in full swing.

What's going on here? How can two supposedly mature adults, one of whom has lectured on stress and humor for 20 years and the other who has been married to a stress-management consultant for 16 years, become so irrational, so upset, so humorless while starting on a vacation, purportedly to relax?

Part of the answer lies in Bob's "musterbating," a term the psychologist Albert Ellis coined that indicates a perspective that things must happen in a certain way. Bob couldn't see other than one way to handle the toll situation. Because of his background, which was filled with rules and regulations, Bob needs to be perfect—that is, *three one-dollar bills*. When I won't play along, he becomes a martyr—"You don't take me seriously"—or he inflicts blame—"You're embarrassing me." As he becomes angry, I fall into my patterned responses. As a child, I, too, was raised to be perfect. When Bob yells or blames, I feel that I'm not perfect. And I deal with this by becoming caustic and bringing up my endless list of things that I've done right.

xv

Fortunately, years of exploring how to handle stress enabled me to get back on track and laugh at our silly argument. The next day, as the deep blue water washed across the sand, we both realized, "What's the point of arguing?" and started to have fun.

Many of us feel exhausted, burned out, and ill from all of the demands and pressures in our lives. We think that the stress we experience comes primarily from the external world, in the form of corporate downsizing and outsourcing, call waiting, two-career families, violence and crime, cell phones, information overload, and millions of images of perfect men and women with perfect faces and figures. However, most stress really comes from how we interpret, label, and judge our world. Things can be good, bad, painful, or pleasant, depending upon your inner criteria.

Since childhood, we have heard our families, friends, and media tell us how to think. When Bob and I were arguing, responses were colored by groups of people that had taken up timesharing in our minds. Our stress levels drop considerably when we begin to evict some of these tenants and learn to think independently.

xvi

At the root of my, Bob's, and most other people's stress are false expectations, ridiculous goals, unrealistic ideas, lack of personal responsibility, and the need to blame someone or something else for our problems in life. Usually we can handle stress with a large dollop of common sense, an ability to see things as they really are, and humor to bring back our perspective when we've blown things out of proportion.

In this book, I want to help you discover that stress—the very thing that creates so much trouble for you—can also be the source of enormous humor and enjoyment. Yes, you can actually use stress as an opportunity for growth, resiliency, and humor. In a phrase, "*stressed is desserts spelled backward*." You can learn to use humor to reframe a stressful situation—that is, to think about it in a different way. This new perspective will enable you to learn to see humor in some of the difficult parts of life.

When most of us hear the word *stress,* we think: negative, harmful, awful. But stress is both positive and negative. There are plenty of things that stress does for us that are necessary. If you felt no stress, you'd be a blob. You wouldn't get out of bed; you'd just be lying there. *No reason to go anywhere; I'll just stay here.*

If you were in a car going 40 miles per hour, and all of a sudden another car jumped the median strip and came head-on toward you, you'd need to feel a little stress. You want to avert a disaster at all costs, so your mind and body say: "Oh my God, do something fast!" Your heart starts palpitating. You say, "Oh man, I'm outta here." This thought can be a lifesaver. However, stress is harmful when we misinterpret the signals. It's really *distress* that we must become aware of. Reacting to being stuck in traffic as if we were being held hostage by a sniper is called overreacting.

xvii

One way to defuse distress is to look at parts of your life as a sitcom, with you as the star. You can watch Jerry Seinfeld, George, Kramer, and Elaine for laughs, but you also can plug into your own sitcom anytime, anywhere. You're your own entertainment center; all you have to do is show up. Most of us don't show up because our minds are so cluttered with things we have to do, we're not present to witness our own comedy. However, once you acquire (or actually reacquire) a humorous attitude toward life, you become part of an Internet of lunacy without needing a computer or a modem.

Find the Bless in the Mess

The Western mind likes to hold off on being happy. How often have you heard these comments: "I'll be happy when I lose weight, when I get divorced, when I retire, when the kids leave . . ." Trust me, they never leave! The most you can hope for is that they'll marry people they deserve.

Our culture is primarily pathological. Too often we focus on what's wrong with people, not what's right. Our absence of heroic, virtuous individuals is a telltale sign of a culture that values perversity rather than purity. I often hear kids say, "He's sooo bad." If bad is good, then good must not be desirable.

You probably already know in great detail why your life doesn't work. Yet we need to challenge ourselves to move away from the safe and familiar worlds of our problems and develop skills that help to see our problems as opportunities—in other words, to see the bless in the mess.

I have been privileged over the years to meet many unsung heroes—individuals who have been tested beyond anything most of us can imagine. I'll never forget one man in particular who had Lou Gehrig's disease. Two aides at his side, he sat in his wheelchair and smiled at me throughout my presentation. Afterward his wife, who helped interpret for him, told me how happy he was to have attended my lecture and how blessed he felt to have his wife and others help him in his hour of need.

Driving home, I had flashbacks of incidents where I turned a hangnail into a *Grey's Anatomy* segment. I know I'm not the only one who does that; otherwise, I wouldn't be in business. But we all need to learn how to turn this kind of negativity around. How about taking the sting out of stress by accepting what you can't change, changing what you can, and laughing at the rest?

You can find the bless in the mess when you're standing in long lines. According to a study conducted by a major university, you're going to spend three years of your life waiting in lines. Why not consider the fact that while you're waiting, you don't have to do anything, and no one can find you! When you're having an argument with your significant other, think how challenging this is to your problem-solving capabilities. If your child keeps you up at night, exult in the fact that you get the opportunity to extend your day. Tape up the following poem by Emily Dickinson. It will help you get through your days and nights with more dignity and grace:

> *Hope is the thing with feathers*
> *That perches in the soul.*
> *And sings the tune without the words*
> *And never stops at all.*

As a stress consultant and lecturer, I have 20 years' experience in helping people (both individuals and members of corporations) find the bless in the mess. I show my clients how to use humor to detoxify and de-stress their relationships and their ways of looking at their jobs, their lives, and their places in the cosmic scheme of things. In fact, since stress is now a multimillion-dollar business, I'm never going to be out of work!

Life's changing conditions are inevitable. There are no guarantees that anything will remain the same, no matter how much we wish it would. So many of the messages we receive would have us believe that pain, suffering, unhappiness, the undesirable shape of certain body parts, and everyday irritations can be held at bay with special products, constant shouts of "This is not fair!" and the entitlement factor ("I deserve" or "I didn't get enough and I need more"). This might be cute when you're 3, but when you're 30, it's time to trade in Romper Room for a reality check.

I'm always reminding people that the one constant you can be sure of is that things happen, and usually when you're not in the mood for them. After recounting a stressful event, individuals often remark to me that they weren't in the mood for what happened. Well, who is? Is there a particular frame of mind that is more receptive to something bad happening? Do we wake up thinking "Wow, I'm really in the mood to get a cold today," or for our homes to go up in flames?

One of the greatest gifts you can give yourself is the recognition that you are not the center of the universe. No one has chosen you in particular as the person most likely to have stressful events foisted upon him or her. No particular person has been appointed to disturb you. This epiphany allows us to begin to let go of the chain-gang mentality—the feeling that we are tethered to a no-option, no-choice life, imprisoned until someone frees us. It also allows us to let go of being a martyr, the Sister of Perpetual Responsibility, and to give up the kingdom of control.

These fundamental principles will enhance your ties to your fellow humans. They will allow you to become more forgiving of yourself and others, to be less judgmental, and more compassionate and understanding. The art of joyful living is most accessible to those who seek to share their strengths and weaknesses with others in the celebration of their essential humanness.

It is therefore important to do the following in order to lead a life that doesn't feel like a stress rehearsal:

1. Live as if you have a full cup. We've all heard that the cup is either half empty or half full. I started to ponder this little metaphor when I heard it for the zillionth time and I thought, *Why would I want either of those options?* If you went to someone's house and they gave you half

a cup of water, your first thought would probably be "Boy, are they cheap!" Yet we perceive our lives in this manner. How about a full cup? What about "my cup runneth over"? I may even have to mop some up! Now you're coming from a feeling of abundance. Your cup will always be full if you begin to consider the ordinary delights and blessings that are simply a part of the universe. Don't make a trip to the mall a criteria for having a full cup.

2. Become well used. We often hear people say, "I feel so used." It's important to differentiate between someone trying to manipulate us and manipulating ourselves to use every ounce of our potential. We need to use our talents, our possibilities, and our hearts to the fullest so that at the end of our lives, when people are gathered to reminisce about us, they will share in the glory of who we were.

3. Use self-parody to remind yourself of how funny you can be, particularly when you get serious about things that aren't essential to your next breath. Try to reach for the highest form of humor, which psychologist Abraham Maslow stated is "to laugh at what you

hold sacred and still hold it sacred."
I realize that there are situations that
we absolutely must take seriously;
however, there is quite a difference
between man's inhumanity to man
and someone having 12 items in the
8-item line.

4. Last but not least, become friends with
    your mortality. We're not getting out of
    here alive! It's very difficult to imagine
    our own demise, but those who have
    fully confronted this and made peace
    with it delight in the precious moments
    they are given, rather than postponing
    and missing the life that exists.

As you read this book, keep in mind a saying
that I use to close my lectures:

> *Yesterday is history.*
> *Tomorrow is a mystery.*
> *And today is a gift. That's why*
> *it's called "the present."*

There is no more important gift that I can give
you than this idea. Sit back and read on.

❧ ❧ ❧   ❧ ❧ ❧

CHAPTER 1

FOUR HUNDRED
TIMES A DAY

Recently I stayed with a friend who had three children, ages two, five, and seven. At breakfast, she took out six different boxes of cereal and began the following litany, first addressing the two-year-old: "Do you want fruit doodles, oat squares, shredded wheat, captain crackles, Trix, or Cheerios? I can put a banana, apple, orange, kiwi, or pineapple on top. I can cut them in halves, thirds, quarters, or mash them. You can have it in a bowl, a soup tureen, a trough, or the dog's dish. Would you like to eat it in your room, at the kitchen table, under the chair, or outside in the bird bath?"

This entire speech took about 15 minutes. During the presentation, the child squirmed, drifted off into a dazed stare, and left the room once or twice. Finally she looked up at her mother and said, "I want a marshmallow." Whereby the mother, confronted with a choice she hadn't expected, began to explain how sorry she was for not having thought about buying marshmallows, and how she was a bad mommy for neglecting to do this. Meanwhile, the other two kids were beating the hell out of each other.

As a child, when I was told it was time for breakfast, I would sit down at the table and eat whatever was placed in front of me. It was oatmeal, an egg that seemed to have a life of its own, or toast, fruit, and milk. My mother was the decision maker. If I started arguing with her, saying I couldn't stand the egg, or "Jessica (my friend down the street) gets peanut butter on toast for breakfast," she'd go into her Sicilian warrior stance. She'd put her hand sideways into her mouth and bite down. This was not a pretty picture. Then she'd growl, "I'll give you what Jessica eats for breakfast." End of discussion. A Sicilian woman biting herself would make George Foreman drop to his knees and beg for mercy.

With all the choices we offer our children today, we're squelching their little spirits. What child really wants six selections of cereal for breakfast? She'd probably enjoy anything you gave her because she's able to be in the moment—something most of us have long forgotten about in our attempt to get things over with.

In addition to being in the moment, children are also prolific at laughter. Stanford professor of psychiatry Dr. William Fry has found that a five-year-old child laughs more than four hundred times a day. But by the time people are adults, that total shrivels to 14 times daily—or less. What happens is that as children grow up, they are told to "get serious." The result is that most adults suffer from terminal seriousness.

How sad it is to realize that the silly and fun in us comes out rarely, and that children who hear an adult tell them to stop behaving foolishly receive many a mixed message. Then they watch that same person behave the same way, only after having a few drinks!

Now, I'm not saying you're going to march around like a wound-up happy doll. This denies our ability to react to different situations with a variety of emotions. But if you don't have to suffer, don't practice! There's plenty of suffering to go around, and we will all get our share.

3

Drop the Change

One of the most widely sold drugs in the U.S. is laxatives. Is this merely a result of our not eating enough fiber, or does a constipated mind have the same consequences? Many of us have become terminally serious or, more to the point, anal retentive. This is a condition that makes us look like we're holding quarters between our cheeks. Some people even look like they're holding dimes. The end result of this condition is that even if we wanted to let out a good laugh, we couldn't, because we can't squeeze and laugh at the same time. Children belly laugh because they haven't started squeezing yet.

In every seminar I do, I ask people to go through a belly laugh with me, to remind them what it feels like to really let go. I take them through the facial expressions; I tell them to open their eyes wide, to lift their eyebrows, grab hold of their bellies (whichever section they like best), and on the count of three, to let fly a HA-HA-HA, which we do for 30 seconds.

When I announce that we're going to do this, the moans and groans that escape most people's lips would make outsiders listening in think these folks are about to be punished. Some people actually note the time before they start, to make sure they get it right—a sure sign of anal retention. Many people look around to see if anyone else is doing it, because, after all, there are reporters from major publications present who, lacking anything else of interest to report, are there to focus on them and the fact that they might be acting silly. (The word *silly*, by the way, comes from the ancient English word *selig*, which means "to be blessed." Many a pompous court was lightened up by the court jester, who was the blessed fool.)

Several times I've had the opportunity to do this exercise with children. One incident in particular has always stuck with me. Years ago, my now 21-year-old grandson Tyler, who used to live outside of Atlanta, asked me to visit his third-grade class and tell them what I do for a living. After I did, I asked them to try the belly laugh for 30 seconds. Immediately they started shouting, "We can do that for an hour!" Their unbridled laughter filled the room. They grabbed their stomachs without any coaching from me, and many of them literally doubled over or fell on the floor, completely capturing the moment. The more they laughed, the more they laughed.

However, it took only a minute or so before the teacher began to look worried. Before long she started saying, "Now, boys and girls, we need to calm down and control ourselves." Although I realize the need for control in the classroom and beyond is a necessary part of a civilized society, there is also the need to release and let go. Many adults say their faces hurt after they leave my workshops, or that their stomachs are killing them. Perhaps many of us are control freaks because we've been told so many times to control ourselves that even the thought of a few minutes of enjoyment can literally cause us pain.

Why is laughter causing us physical pain? I've never seen a group of four-year-olds who were giggling like mad stop so they could report to some adult that their faces hurt and they just couldn't take any more. Our faces hurt because the muscles that help us laugh are out of shape.

The Joy of Stress

One of the tenets of Buddhism states that pain and pleasure are two sides of the same coin. And in the theater, tragedy and comedy are always interconnected. So it makes sense that we should be able to turn a negative situation into a positive one if we are able to look at it differently, realizing that we can draw humor or gain valuable insights from something that initially appears to be annoying, sad, or even devastating.

What's so joyful about stress? What's so joyful about being in the grocery store line behind a lady who has 100 coupons so she can get 20 cents off a loaf of bread? About kids who miss the school bus every morning, so you can drive them? About living with someone who won't read their relationship dictionary? Each of us has the power to decide how to interpret stressful events: with humor, with wisdom, with compassion, or with the willingness to accept the situation for what it is.

Since stress is an essential part of life, we're all going to worry to some extent—whether it's about aging, making our mortgage payments, or downsizing. But you can determine how much you let stress take over and how much you control it. Right now I want to debunk some myths about stress.

— **Myth 1:** *Stress is the same for everybody.* Stress is different for each of us. What is stressful for one person may or may not be stressful for another person. For instance, having people over for dinner is stressful for some of us, but for others, it's relaxing and fun. Perception is everything!

— **Myth 2:** *Stress is always bad for you.* This is wrong also. Stress is to life what tension is to the violin string: too little, and the music is dull and raspy; too much, and the music is shrill or the string snaps. Stress can be the kiss of death or the spice of life. The issue is how to manage it.

— **Myth 3:** *Stress is everywhere, so you can't do anything about it.* Not so. You can do something about it, including taking a humorous approach to lighten the burden and give you the perspective to make rational plans to deal with stress.

7

— **Myth 4:** *No symptoms, no stress.* Don't be fooled. An absence of symptoms doesn't mean an absence of stress. In fact, camouflaging symptoms with medication may deprive people of the signals they need to reduce their stress.

— **Myth 5:** *Only major symptoms of stress require attention.* "Minor" symptoms, such as headaches, backaches, or heartburn, should not be ignored. They are early warnings that your life is getting out of hand.

Realize that stress and worry are a part of life, but don't become such a worrier that it keeps you from enjoying yourself. A lack of humor in your life can lead to depression. Then you're not laughing at all, and they take you away and put you in rehab. Then you get into group therapy, where you color and make baskets. When you can laugh again, they send you home.

The Body-Whine Connection

8

My belief in the power of humor and joyful living to relieve stress is based not only on these centuries-old notions but on cutting-edge science. In recent years, researchers have shown that laughter positively affects the body in a number of ways:

- The body temperature rises, making you feel warmer.

- The pulse and blood pressure drop.

- Muscles contract, then relax as you laugh.

- Breathing becomes deeper.

- Serum oxygen levels are elevated, which benefits the cardiovascular system, heightens energy levels, and reduces tension.

Laughter also boosts your immune system. It activates T lymphocytes and natural killer cells, both of which help destroy invading microorganisms. In addition, laughter increases the production of immunity-boosting gamma interferon and speeds up the production of new immune cells. And it reduces levels of the stress hormone cortisol, which can weaken the immune system. It appears that when we laugh, we release endorphins, which are chemical cousins to the opiates heroin and morphine, natural painkillers.

And a robust laugh gives your diaphragm, thorax, abdomen, heart, lungs, and maybe even the liver a good workout. Dr. Fry discovered that laughing for 10 minutes is similar to rowing on a rowing machine 100 times. Your muscles tighten and relax, and thereby grow stronger. Thanks to a pulmonary cardiac reflex, your pulse can double from, say, 60 to 120. Laughing is aerobic; laughing with gusto turns your body into a big vibrator and performs an internal massage. This could be safe sex at its best!

9

As with sex, this arousal leaves you more relaxed. Your skin is more sensitive; your muscles, having been exercised, have gone slack with rest. Tears of laughter have left your eyes glistening, and your cortisol level has been reduced, thereby strengthening your immune system. You may even laugh so hard you wet your pants—a sure sign of letting go. Laughter may be the closest thing to an orgasm. That certainly speaks to safe "sex."

One of the best ways to protect the heart is to laugh often and exuberantly, even in situations that you might find unfunny or irritating. Michael Miller, M.D., director of the Center for Preventive Cardiology at the University of Maryland Medical Center, Baltimore, found that heart patients were 40 percent less likely than their healthy counterparts to laugh in a variety of common situations. "The old axiom that 'laughter is the best medicine' appears to hold true when it comes to protecting your heart," states Dr. Miller.

A good paradigm shift is if we can realize that the moment we're living in is the only moment there is. We can shout to the rooftops "I'm glad to be alive!" Maybe things in the universe would change if we all went in to work and said this. Being in the moment gives you the ability to handle life's imperfections. Hey, this is what exists—it's not such a big deal.

10

We need to adopt a philosophy of living a joyous life every day. This is the best buffer against stress that I know of. Most people compartmentalize enjoyment, reserving it for weekends, birthdays, or holidays. I believe that you should live life as if you have only a few minutes left. The hats, horns, confetti, and champagne that you save for New Year's Eve should be at your side every day. Revel in the accomplishments you achieve and in the kindnesses you receive. Celebrate the moments, hours, and minutes of your existence. As you do, you'll leave behind a life filled with "Oh no's" and awake to one overflowing with "Aha's!"

The Committee

Most people never realize that even when they're alone, they have a group traveling with them. I call it the Committee. The Committee was in full attendance when Bob and I battled it out on our way to the beach. This group consists of your parents, other family members, children, and others who have meant something to you in your life—teachers, coaches, ex-lovers, and former spouses, for instance.

Committee members provided you with powerful messages about yourself and the world. Some messages are positive, rational, and protective: Don't put your hand on the stove; look both ways before you cross the street; get dressed before you leave the house; hard work is the key to success. Other messages are negative, irrational, and hurtful: Make your bed every day; wear clean underwear because you never know when you'll be in an accident; you don't deserve affection unless you get straight A's in school. If you consider that we hear almost 350,000 "no's" by the time we reach the age of three, is it any wonder that we turn out to be negative?

If you continue to believe these negative messages when you grow up, you'll live a life filled with stress because you'll think in a rigid and unreflective manner. Do you really feel that if you don't make your bed, bed-checkers will show up and report you? If you are in an accident, is your

11

underwear going to stay clean anyway? And how many people actually do get straight A's? Are the rest of us unlovable because we failed to do these things?

The Committee blares out many other messages throughout your childhood, such as:

- Clean your room, and then you can play. (What a treat. Why can't we clean and play at the same time?)

- Don't leave any dishes in the sink. (Take them with you—then no one will find them.)

- Wipe that stupid grin off your face. (Is there a smart grin?)

- When are you going to grow up? (Hopefully, never.)

- If only you were more like your sister, you wouldn't do that. (Thank God, I'm me. Aren't I lucky?)

Usually there is one individual who issues the Committee's "annual report" and announces new areas for criticism. In my case, it was my mother.

12

My Mother, the CEO

I was born in Brooklyn, into a big Italian family. The head of my Committee, its CEO, CFO, and lifetime board member, is my mother. Admittedly, my mom had a lot to deal with; she was divorced when I was seven, and after that I became the driving force in her life. She wanted me to turn out well and succeed, so she could be proud of me.

Her main message throughout my childhood was that I needed to behave perfectly. Whenever my mother wanted me to clean my room or get better grades, she would always add, "You never know." She never finished the sentence, but the admonishment worked because it induced fear. She planted doubt in my mind: "If I don't do what she wants, maybe something bad will happen." You had to make your bed, or she'd say, "You never know." What if someone stops by and looks into your bedroom? What if the bed-checkers come over? And you had to wear clean underwear, in case you were in an accident. Let's face it—your underwear isn't going to stay clean for long if you're in an accident.

Another of my mother's great messages is saving for a rainy day. This continues even until now. Growing up, no one could sit at the table and use the good dishes. We ate off the chipped china and drank out of jelly glasses. Only people we didn't know could use the good china. We don't know who you are, but you can use the good dishes!

13

Now that my mother is 96, she says she's saving them for me. But as time goes by, the chances of me being able to see the pattern are going from slim to none.

This attitude carried through into other areas. When I'd visit, she always told me not to sit in the living room because she just cleaned it. No problem, I'll just sit in the filthy room. As a kid, I had a pair of underpants my mother didn't let me wear because they were too good. My mother called them my "party pants." I still have them— they just don't fit anymore.

14

Like my mother, millions of people have deluded themselves into thinking that they have to wait for a special occasion to enjoy their lives. Have you ever been to a funeral where people are talking about how fabulous the deceased looks? That's because somebody finally went to her closet, got her good outfit, and put it on her, including her party pants. Then all her friends went back to her house to eat off the good dishes and sit in her clean living room. At last, a special occasion!

Trustees

Trustees on my Committee include nuns from my Catholic schools and my grandfather and grandmother.

The nuns did give me a good education, but many of their messages filled me with guilt. I often heard as a child, "That will go on your permanent record." The permanent record always contained your misdeeds, never your accomplishments. The implication was clear—at least to me. Someone knows the bad things you've done, and he's saving it until the end of time, and beyond.

Another trustee, my grandmother Francesca, added in the need to suffer. Francesca walked around heaving huge Sicilian sighs of despair, sweeping her hand up to her forehead, uttering phrases of doom and gloom with a great deal of drama. Joy, she felt, was irresponsible. Her goal was to report all the misery in her life. Favorites were the weather (it was never right); buying food (they were trying to rob her); and relatives (the years of shame her mother caused by marrying a younger man). Francesca believed we're guaranteed a place in heaven if we go around feeling like hell. My grandmother wanted us to think she never enjoyed herself. So she ate sparingly and complained about her frequent bouts of insomnia with the dramatic flair of an Academy Award winner.

15

There was, however, a flip side to my child-hood—just as in most people's childhoods. Every-one was always hugging, yelling, and cooking—not necessarily in that order. If we weren't eating, we were planning what we'd eat next. There was a passion for life and a raucous humor, and my family adjusted to daily calamities with courage, strength, and resiliency. They had tremendous endurance and an unwillingness to be pitied.

There were tragedies, obstacles to be overcome, and complaints both real and imagined, but there was always laughter. It filtered in and out of our lives, gave us a sense of control over situations, and provided a feeling of hope that things would work out.

My grandfather Lorenzo was a master at reversing stressful situations and an optimist to boot—even though Francesca wouldn't allow much happiness. He had lost an arm prior to my birth, but he didn't seem to notice. Lorenzo would often approach people who were having a problem opening a door or picking up a bundle and offer his services. "Let me do that for you," he would say. They would be delighted. He would later tell me they had problems because they had two arms. Lorenzo's mission statement about life was simple: Live and let live, laugh at yourself and the predicaments you've gotten yourself into, and have a glass of wine and a plate of spaghetti every day.

16

Although times were tough and food scarce, my grandfather would always put a positive spin on everything. "Tonight we are having lamb stew without the lamb," he would announce. Lorenzo would then pick up his glass of wine and toast the yet uncooked food. Francesca would say, "Your eyes are going to get very small from drinking that wine."

The glue of life is loving support from our family and our community, and this is missing from a lot of our lives today. Studies have shown that living with extended family increases longevity. These aged aunts, uncles, and grandparents never ate low-fat food or exercised, and they lived into their upper 80s. How many of us live with extended family today? We don't even live in the same towns any more. Now most of us get out of our parents' homes and want to be alone—we want to have our "space."

When is the last time someone brought you a cake, just because you moved into the neighborhood? If they did, you'd probably cut it open to see if there was a razor blade buried in it. We've lost our sense of community today. We don't even know the owners of the places we shop in.

Back when I was growing up, when we went food shopping, we knew everyone. When we went to the cheese shop, they gave us cheese to taste. No one gives you cheese today because someone from the Cheese Alert Squad would report it. I'd go with Francesca to the chicken lady. She looked like she was related to her chickens. Francesca would look into the chicken's eyes, and touch it and squeeze it. She wouldn't take it home until she'd fondled it. Nowadays, you go into a store, and it's just a corpse in a Styrofoam coffin.

Today you can't even enjoy your food. There's always someone from the low-fat police at your table. "How many grams do you think are in that? Your cholesterol's going to go up!" We need to enjoy our food as a pleasure. Low-fat food isn't healthful if I get pissed off while I'm eating it. I'll discuss this

17

more later, but having pleasure does make your immune system better.

Keep It Simple

Despite all the yelling, hugging, and cooking, our house used to be quiet at times. Now it's always the phone or the answering machine. People get home and head right for the machine. "Do I have a message? I hope I have a message!" We hope we have a message so we won't feel insignificant.

18

Back then my grandparents had very simple conversations. "Wanna go to bed?" "Sure." "Wanna eat something?" "Sure, why not?" My grandmother had five kids, and I don't think she even knew where they came from. Now you're supposed to coach the other person about sex. We've gone over the edge; we don't take anything—even sex—at face value any more.

Growing up, music used to lift our spirits. We used to listen to classical music and show tunes, with great lyrics and melodies. Now people listen to music that I'm sure has been recorded in the depths of hell. And it's a proven fact that noise pollution can stress you out.

Unfortunately, all these changes in our society have reinforced the trend toward negativity. We know that the mind seems to retain more of the negative comments it receives than the positive ones. I believe much of this comes from a societal belief that you ward off pain and unhappiness by hedging your bets with a good dose of negative affirmations. For instance, my husband, Bob, is always worried about Them. He comes from a conservative New England family that is concerned about what others say and think. He can never understand how I can talk to perfect strangers when I'm standing in lines, or how I could possibly go out to get the newspaper in my bathrobe.

Since I'm always trying to fix or cure everyone, I periodically try to dislodge Them from Bob's Committee. Little kids love to run around naked, and often dance in the buff. I thought, *Now, this is something I should try.* So one night I greeted Bob at the door wearing nothing but his wing-tipped shoes. I was laughing hysterically about how I looked. Bob didn't crack a smile. Instead, he bellowed, "What are the neighbors going to think?"

"I don't know," I replied. "I haven't shown them yet."

Get Off the Bus

People spend years in analysis, trying to identify and find rational ways to handle their Committees. I've been very fortunate in that the humor I inherited helps me break through the irrational thoughts that come with the Committee's messages. Much of what I thought was absolute, I now find absurd. This gives me peace of mind, more

19

time to pursue pleasure, and less inclination to be on anyone else's Committee. I'd like to share one of my favorite ways of helping people free themselves from their Committees.

Imagine that your mind is like a big bus. Put on board everyone from your Committee and take them for a ride: your parents, your aunt, your third-grade teacher, your basketball coach, your minister. Look in the mirror in the morning and say, "*I'm* driving the bus! I don't think I'll wear underpants today, and I'm not making my bed either!"

You are the only one who can make yourself happy. The responsibility is up to you. I learned this late in life, and the power I've gained from that bit of wisdom is phenomenal. For example, I love it when my husband comes home for dinner—and I love it when he doesn't. Either way, I enjoy myself. As long as I show up, I'll have fun!

Stinking Thinking

Much of our stress and emotional suffering comes from the way we think. I'm a master of this; I can drive myself nuts in two minutes. The thoughts that cause us stress are usually negative, unrealistic, and distorted. They're knee-jerk automatic responses that just pop out. You're in the parking lot—aha! They took all the spaces! It's a

20

plot; we think that people get up before we do, go to the parking lot, and put their cars in our spaces.

Let's say you go to the movies. You've got to get the right seat with no one in front of you. People come in and they're also looking for the right seat. They sit in front of you, and one has a big head. You start to think, *Oh no! Oh my God, not again. Why me? Why do I always get the people with big heads? This always happens to me! Now I won't see a thing. My whole night is ruined!* You took a simple thing, distorted it in your mind, and ruined the whole night for yourself. The thought that you could move, or accept the situation, thereby solving the problem, doesn't even enter your head. It always fascinates me that we would rather make things worse than make them better.

Even though I lecture, write, and read everything on relieving stress that I can get my hands on, I still periodically get sucked into my nutty-putty mentality. It usually happens when I'm in a rush and haven't prepared adequately in advance. Recently I had to tape a program for a client, and was told to arrive at 9:30 A.M. I had time the night before to get my clothing ready, but oh no, I decided to get up early and do it then. I had, however, made up my mind about what I was going to wear. And you know how that is. You have made a decision that is set in stone. Not even a petition from the Pope could change it.

21

Eventually I did find the suit, but then it came time to find the shoes. The bottom of my closet would make a snake pit appear charming. I began searching calmly, but with each passing minute I began to exhibit telltale signs that a bloodbath was about to ensue. Shoes started flying as I desperately searched for the right pair. I was rewarded at last, but there was only one. "I knew it," I shouted, "it's gone!" Of course, I added, "Someone took it!" Meanwhile, my time of departure was getting closer, but I was on a mission that was similar to finding the Holy Grail. I *would* find that shoe! Nothing else mattered at this point.

22

It also became important to find out who took the shoe. Now, there's no one else living at my house except my husband and me, so guess what? It had to be him—he took it. Did it ever occur to me while I was in this complete state of frenzy that a 6'3" man with a size-12 shoe would not only not fit into a size-7 pump, but that what in God's name would he want with one shoe with a stacked heel? It didn't even match any of his suits. I was finally saved by the absurd image that came to me of my husband trying to get the shoe on. I shared this story with several people who could all relate. It's amazing how many of us are doing the same things and how upset we make ourselves.

Millions of people rush home every night to watch their favorite sitcoms, either to get relief from feeling overwhelmed or perhaps just to get a dose of the giggles. But, as I said earlier, you don't need the television set. You're only a thought away from starring in your own sitcom. All you have to do is tap into the internal dialogue that runs through your mind every day. It is filled with irrational statements, the mother lode of comedy.

The psychological terminology for these irrational statements is cognitive distortions. In their 12-step program, Alcoholics Anonymous calls it "stinking thinking." If you're in therapy or you're taking a course in stress management, a great deal of emphasis is placed on how you think.

This sounds like common sense, doesn't it? But how many of us really understand this principle—that your thoughts create your feelings, and your feelings create your behavior? Just to test this theory, try throwing your arms up in the air, jumping up and down, and yelling: "I'm depressed!" It just doesn't work.

23

Whether you're feeling angry, sad, or happy, your mind is conducting the outcome. You're an orchestra of chemical responses that plays the same tune over and over again. How many people commute to work acting as if they are playing *The 1812 Overture?* Have you ever noticed how some people drive? Some folks drive in a happy way—"Whew! I got there." These people want to live. Some people have to say something about the traffic. "Damn it! Jackasses! Where did they get their licenses from? Where did all these cars come from?" This thought is totally irrational. So is the behavior that usually follows: a string of expletives, clenched fingers on the wheel, and eyes nearly popping out of their heads. Aside from their looking like Looney Tunes characters, there's a serious misunderstanding of reality going on here.

Fight or Flight

Almost every day we blow things out of proportion and put the most negative spin on events in our lives. Too much "catastrophizing" and "awfulizing" triggers a physiological response called "fight or flight," the engine that drives much of our stress. Walter B. Cannon, a psychiatrist at Harvard at the turn of the century, described the fight-or-flight response as a series of biochemical changes that prepare us to deal with threats. This was a great idea about a million years ago, when people had to defend themselves against saber-toothed tigers or wooly behemoths. However, flash forward to shortly before the end of the 20th century and to any major highway. You're in your car in a traffic jam and you're yelling at people who can't hear you. You are using a response that is no longer useful.

Since the body doesn't know whether it's in a cave or in a car, it responds to what it thinks are your cries for help. Your eyes get narrow to see farther, and your hearing gets more acute in case the animal leaves its vehicle. Your heart rate, blood volume, and blood pressure all go up. You start to

24

perspire. Your hands and feet get cold as blood is directed away from your extremities and digestive system into larger muscles that help you fight or run. Your diaphragm and anus lock. Nature is very wise: It prepares you just in case you're going to scare the living crap out of yourself.

In your car, you reach for your "spear"—usually your middle finger or a choice obscenity. In front of you is a 78-year-old woman in a Buick. She's enjoying her day, driving slowly, because wisdom has taught her that at her age, what's the rush? She doesn't realize that in back of her is a raving Neanderthal who perceives her to be a Behemoth.

How many times a day do you get ready to throw a "spear"? How many minutes, hours, or days of your life are you uttering dialogue appropriate for battle rather than for a Xerox machine that won't work, a line that's too long, a haircut that came out too short, or a child who won't listen? Virtually anything can trigger the fight-or-flight response if you interpret the situation as harmful or threatening.

Life becomes unbearably stressful when you make faulty conclusions about your world. It is *your* interpretations about experiences that create anxiety, anger, and depression. When you decide that a wet towel left on a bed is an offense similar to a mugging, you are creating a stormy emotional climate for yourself, one that will lead to enormous stress in your life. Chronically enacting the fight-or-flight response can hurt you physically

25

and emotionally a great deal, affecting virtually every part of your body.

As I said earlier, one of the most dangerous by-products of stress in the body is cortisol. A host of dangerous situations can arise if your body is producing cortisol continually because of your reactions to stress, problems such as a debilitated immune system, blood clots, or a heart attack or stroke.

Some of us have illnesses that we don't realize are stress related. Headaches aren't a normal part of life. It's not as if you were born with a headache.

You start getting headaches because the vessels around your head begin squeezing. Often people hold tension in the neck and back, creating stiffness there and culminating in a thundering headache. In fact, many people think having headaches and backaches is normal, and without them, they wouldn't be accomplishing much. People even compare their aches and pains: "I've had a headache all day!" "I've had five headaches!" "Good, you win. You get a bottle of Advil and a trip to the neurologist."

Many of us go to bed at night, and we just can't let things go. A lot of times we lie in bed reviewing. We should be able to think about something once, and that's it. But the mind doesn't know when to shut up, does it? There's a yakety-yak effect going on in our heads all day; researchers say that 60,000 thoughts pass through the average person's brain daily. If you don't know how to shut them off,

26

you're going to experience the fight-or-flight reaction when you're trying to go to sleep.

If stress continues with no relief, it can even kill us. A *60 Minutes* program showed that many Japanese employees were actually dropping dead at their desks from working 16-hour days, day in and day out. We Americans also push ourselves too hard at work. What we all need to understand is that if something happens to you, you will be replaced at your company. The office will open the next day without you. Someone else will take your job, and you'll be in the cemetery while they're sitting in your seat at meetings. How many funerals have you been to where people are discussing how many times the dead person worked late at the office?

27

It's amazing to me that most doctors don't even consider the manifestations of stress. They never ask, "What's your life like? How do you feel about your work? How do you feel about your marriage? Are you eating properly, and are you exercising?" All they ask is when you had the measles! That has a lot to do with the headache I have today, doesn't it? And yet, according to a Harvard study, from 60 to 90 percent of office visits to primary care physicians are stress-related due to lifestyle.

Often we react to the stress we encounter with negative, self-defeating thoughts. Our stinking thinking comes from our need to support and sustain our self-esteem, as a result of messages we've gotten from our Committees. These negative thoughts habitually pop into our minds, uninvited, rather than as a result of reasoning.

We've inherited and continue to believe hundreds of cognitive distortions that leave us feeling crazed, humorless, and out of control. This lemming philosophy denies us the ability to question our Committee members, even though they may be dead or senile.

The root of these irrational thought patterns is exaggeration. Interestingly enough, this is also the root of humor. We laugh at many of our favorite comedians because they are able to observe our behavior and take it several steps beyond reality until we're able to make the connection and laugh at how truly ridiculous we are. It's more difficult for us to laugh at ourselves because we're invested on many levels in owning, awfulizing, and being right.

Many of us are masters of comedy in our own right, but we just don't get it. Some of the stuff that comes out of our lips is hysterical: "I just can't take it anymore" (Unfortunately, you do until you come up with an alternative.); "I'm only human" (Well, that makes perfect sense if you're talking to a cat!); "No one cares" (How sad, you've concluded that of the billion or so people who inhabit the planet, there isn't one soul who cares about you. The years of researching this fact must have left you exhausted!). Most of our minds are truly a playground of absurdity.

In order to see the humor in anything, you must stand outside yourself in the position of a compassionate witness. From that position, you can create something uplifting out of the situation by seeing the incongruity and silliness in the plight of being human. You can realize that your distorted, irrational thoughts are exaggerations of misinterpreted reality, and you can turn crisis into triumph by laughing in its face. Not because the circumstances are funny, but because, with your conscious mind, you have chosen to see the humor in the situation.

Ta-Dah Today, Tomorrow May Be Too Late

29

Several years ago, while attending a conference on wellness, I was struck by the attitude of the participants. Most approached the sessions, which were focused on how to extend life, with grim earnestness and very little energy. In their relentless pursuit of a healthy, long life, they had forgotten the present.

One afternoon, a child of about three waltzed down the hotel corridor, twirled, lifted her arms, and yelled, "TA-DAH!"

Several adults stopped dead in their tracks. At that instant, I knew they had grasped the absurdity of the situation. The child knew what they had paid hundreds of dollars to find out: how to enjoy life in the moment.

A childlike TA-DAH! blesses the moment you're in. It permits you to enjoy wherever you are and to realize, more often than not, that you *choose* to be there. If you fail to understand this reality, you are forever waiting "to be done" before you can have fun. To my knowledge, I've never seen a tombstone that said: "Did everything, died anyway." The realization that we have already arrived, that we don't have to travel any farther, that we're already here, can give us peace and joy.

There is even a scientific study that has concluded that throwing your arms up into the air can lift your spirits. A study by Dr. John Cacioppo, Ph.D., an Ohio State University psychologist, says it may have something to do with the fact that this upward motion is similar to bringing food to the mouth, an action we instinctively enjoy. The giddy, goofy desire to throw wide your arms and embrace life not only makes life worth living but may make it last longer. Perhaps euphoria is good for the body; perhaps joy is protective against the corrosive impact of stress, and joyful people may outlive their whining counterparts. There is even a yoga pose called Tadasana, which means "stand firm, with power and dignity, steadily and comfortably." And "Todah" in Hebrew means "Thank you."

There are endless possibilities to enjoy our existence. Life's little pleasures too often disappear from our busy days. The absence of ordinary pleasures may take an even greater toll on our health than stress does. So take out the good dishes, go into the clean living room, and eat dessert in your party pants! I've come up with a list of ten TA-DAHs that can take you outside of yourself and heal your negative thoughts:

1. Trade frowns for smiles.
2. Talk to yourself in fun ways.
3. Touch someone else's life.
4. Take time to listen to yourself.
5. Treat yourself to pleasure and passion.
6. Turn on your imagination.
7. Tidy up your life.
8. Tap into the universe of humor.
9. Try to be different.
10. Tolerate more, and give thanks often.

31

Ta-Dah Number One: Trade Frowns for Smiles

It's so easy to frown, and there are so many things to frown at: a stack of bills, a child making noise in a restaurant, a colleague who comes into your office and chats as if you have nothing else to do. But when we take these frown makers and smile at them, a funny thing happens: Our annoyance at the problem tends to go away. The next time you're tempted to frown at someone, grin instead. The person may be taken aback, and you'll be surprised at how your attitude will follow the expression on your face.

Many women spend tons of money on products to enhance our looks and, in particular, our faces. Antiwrinkle creams abound with the magic promises of youth. Mascara, blush, and eye shadow are designed to give our faces a lift. However, have you ever considered the fact that the expression on your face has a lot more to do with having a pleasant exterior than any makeup or lack of wrinkles?

If you were to park your car on a busy street and observe people walking by, you'd see an inordinate amount of stern faces, clenched jaws, and just plain grumpy looks. These uptight faces, in turn, create uptight bodies, which the mind translates into stress. As children, you had from 18 to 20 facial expressions. By the time you became an adult, you were down to four. Since adulthood is supposed to be more serious and important than childhood, being too expressive may make us afraid of appearing foolish. As grown-ups we restrict foolishness, play, and happy faces for vacation or Friday through Sunday evenings.

Smiles, frowns, and grimaces were once seen simply as expressions of feelings. However, researchers now see the face as a body organ of its own. Increasingly, scientists are realizing that facial expressions *precede* feelings and play a role in generating them.

The "Facial Feedback" theory proposes that if you ask a person to smile, she soon begins to experience the pleasant feelings associated with that expression. How? When you smile, two things happen: You breathe through your nose, and you exert pressure on the veins in your face. When you breathe through your nose, you bring air into your nasal passages, which cools the veins and the blood flowing through them. And when you use the "smile muscles" at the corners of your mouth, you change the direction of the blood flow inside your face in such a way that it causes the temperature of the blood to drop. This cooler blood enters the region of the brain known as the hypothalamus and causes the release of chemicals that can suppress pain and help a person feel better.

Cooling the blood may promote the release of endorphins, which, as we discussed earlier, suppress pain and give you a lift. In short, smiling instructs our brains to feel good.

33

The head of plastic surgery at a local hospital told me that as we age, our faces set into a mask. If this is true, it's important to keep our facial muscles flexible by laughing. We need to change the looks on our faces. Kids make silly faces all the time; they're experts at it. I like to make silly faces in elevators. People act like, "Don't touch me, don't come close!" I never face the same way they do; I smile at them and say, "Let's hug!" What are they afraid of, the face police?

A pleasant smile can help you have a relaxed mental state and a healthy body. Why not give it a try—start your day with a happy face. It's free, unlike all that makeup, and you're liable to get a wonderful reaction—someone might smile back.

Smile at your wife, smile at your husband,
smile at your children,
smile at each other, it doesn't matter who it is,
and that will help you
to grow up in greater love for each other.
— Mother Teresa

In the following chapters, we'll have fun together as we observe the thoughts, feelings, and behaviors that create our inability to be more accepting, joyful, and present. And I hope by sharing many of my irrational behaviors that you will become more connected to yours and that we'll be able to look through the lens of humor together. One of the most powerful assets a sense of humor provides us with is the ability to shift perspective and be flexible. Remember that flexibility is the ability not to get bent out of shape.

34

☯ ☯ ☯   ☯ ☯ ☯

CHAPTER 2

THE NEED TO DO EVERYTHING PERFECTLY

When I was younger, I was such a people pleaser. If everyone else was happy, then I could be happy. I was also a perfectionist. Everything had to be done by me personally; everything was done from scratch. I used to clean everything, cook everything, and make everything. There wasn't anything I didn't do or try to do perfectly. People would come to my house and say, "Oh, I love your drapes!" and I'd say, "I made them myself!" "I love your walls!" "I painted them myself!" "I smell bread!" "Baked it myself!" "Are those your children?" "Yeah, I made 'em myself!"

I think of the silly things I said back then, such as "You could eat off my floors." Now, isn't that special? Imagine sending an invitation to come over and eat off my floors!

I was also a slave to rules. I did things and didn't even know why I was doing them. I was cooking a roast beef, and I cut the ends off and threw them away, as I always did. It occurred to me to wonder why, so I called my mother. "Why do we cut the ends off?" I asked. "I don't know, ask your grandmother." So I called Francesca. "I don't know why *you're* doing it," she said. "*I* did it because it didn't fit in the pan."

By now, I'm sick of cooking and cleaning. After 30 years of mopping, scouring, and dusting, I'm seriously considering (if you'll excuse the expression) throwing in the towel. I just don't clean the oven anymore. I've found that if you leave it alone, the oven starts to season the food with its odors. I now have a gourmet oven!

I remember the first time I dusted. I actually begged my mother to allow me to help her. Her clever response: "If you're a good girl, I'll let you dust and polish with lemon oil, too." This was enough to send me into housecleaning heaven. Little did I know that my artful polishing would become a never-ending battle against dirt.

We are a nation possessed with eradicating filth. I've never counted them, but I imagine there are millions of products on the market designed to keep our homes, cars, and bodies clean and sparkling. Personally, I am fed up with their lies.

I've never been obsessed with having sparkling dinnerware. No woman who has eaten at my home has ever turned over a plate and used it as a mirror to apply her lipstick.

I feel the same about cleaning the bathroom. My mother passed on to me rigorous standards for cleanliness in this area. Her admonition to make sure that I cleaned underneath the toilet bowl kept me paranoid for years. Then one day I suddenly realized that nobody that short was ever coming to visit.

I've tried to remove stains from clothing with some of the "miracle" products in stores today and found that most of the time, the color of the cleaner simply became a permanent part of the design of the blouse. The lies about soap powders are the most insidious of all: "Whites whiter than white." What, really, does that mean? And besides, my husband has never gotten a raise because his shirt was extra white.

I've noticed that there is even a new form of guilt that's been added to having clean laundry. Now it's supposed to be soft too. Pictures of people holding towels to their cheeks and cooing with delight abound on TV. My family managed to survive for years with unsoftened towels. I don't recall ever having to take anyone to the emergency room with lacerations after they dried themselves off.

Aside from keeping the house clean, keeping our bodies clean has become a major project. By the time I'm done soaping, rinsing, moisturizing, flossing, brushing, combing, moussing, and deodorizing, I'm ready to go to bed.

I suppose there's no easy solution to cleaning, except to hire someone who isn't sick of it. But then I'd have to clean the house first so the cleaner wouldn't think I was dirty.

I'm not the only one. There was a woman in one of my workshops who told me she had to vacuum the carpet in a certain direction so the nap would lay down properly. Then she'd back out of the room so she wouldn't disturb the nap. I told her, "It's not the nap that's disturbed!"

Food shopping is a chore that I absolutely hate. The last time I opened the refrigerator, its gleaming shelves held one carrot and an apple. But glory be, the empty shelves have finally led my husband to offer to do the weekly shopping. Now I'm letting him do it. So what if he never buys the right brand of toilet paper?

Are you the kind of person who feels you have to Do Everything Perfectly? You are the only person who knows how to do this one thing exactly right. Only you can do it—and you never, ever make mistakes. After all, that would make you human, and we wouldn't want that, would we?

You place unrealistic demands on yourself and others by using words such as *must, need,* and *have to.* This sets you up for "musterbating," one of Bob's favorite activities. As I said earlier, the psychologist Albert Ellis coined the term. He said, "Masturbation is delicious, but musterbating is evil." Musterbating is when you must do something a certain way and things must happen in a certain fashion. We are never able to rest because our Committees have trained us that we must do everything well.

Perfectionism is a kind of stinking thinking that never allows you to rest, because you always think you could have done it better. A good effort doesn't count—the job has to be done exactly the way you would have done it. Also, it's impossible for someone to help you, because you just know he can't do the task like you can. "You'd only be in the way" or "You'd slow me down" is your favorite response to offers of help. Perfectionists tend to criticize others constantly, because, of course, they're not doing things the right way. Perfectionism can lead to frustration and anxiety, since it's an illusion. You can strive for excellence, but you'll never be perfect. You're never satisfied because you always see the imperfections in what you tried to accomplish.

39

The Need to Be Right

The corollary to Doing Everything Perfectly is the Need to Be Right. You're right, you've been right for years, and you can't understand why everyone else doesn't know it. How dare they question you! When you have the need to be right, it's hard to let go. People like this remind me of a small Chihuahua, hanging on to a piece of meat. They won't let go for dear life. They often will say, "Didn't I tell you? I was right, wasn't I?" My question for you is: Do you want to be right, or do you want to be happy?

Here are some ways for perfectionists to move from common sense to nonsense:

1. Make a "not to-do" list: Write down everything you've done already or what you have enough of. For example, "Called Mom, have lots of toilet paper, sent Johnny a birthday card." At the end of the day, go over it and shout, "Look what I did! I'm a regular house of fulfillment!"

2. Make your bed, but don't tuck in one side. Test yourself to see if you can walk away without having an anxiety attack. As you leave the room, tell yourself, *It's okay, they'll never find out.* Eventually train yourself to not make the bed at all one day a week. If you can't even begin to do this, you might want to consider starting a group for Adult Children of Parents Who Can't Stop Making Beds.

3. Tell just one person about one thing that you don't do neatly. Maybe your underwear is not totally lined up, or some of your socks don't have a mate. Begin the process of seeing yourself as someone who is capable of not being perfect.

4. Go outside when it's raining, and get all wet. Try it sometime when you have something "good" on. I realize that

40

this is pushing the envelope, but after the first beads of sweat break out from fear that you may be recognized, you'll probably enjoy yourself.

5. Let someone borrow your good pencil or pen. Try not to think about the fact that it may be ruined. Keep in mind that as long as there are trees on the planet, you'll be able to buy another pencil.

Along with my aforementioned cleaning mania, when I was bringing up my kids, I was possessed with everything looking right. I was in the highest state of hypervigilance; I was a machine tuned to any flaw that might be lurking unseen by other less trained individuals. Of course, I obviously chose to ignore the fact that while they were having fun, I was whiling away the hours searching for dirt and for towels that matched, and redoing things that other people had done.

I started teaching my firstborn son, Jon, how to clean his room as soon as he could walk. His toys had to be put back exactly where they had been. After all, *Martha Stewart Living* has a crew of roving reporters who randomly check children's rooms. Even when he had the program down to a science, I would go in and redo anything that wasn't perfect. Sometimes when Jonnie was making a fort with his blocks, I would saunter in and give suggestions as to where the blocks would really look good. It's amazing that he didn't end up on the *Dr. Phil* show revealing how he had overcome a severe building block disorder to go on to be successful and raise a healthy, happy family. Someone up there must be watching and cutting us some slack, for my son Jon is one of the sweetest, most gentle souls I know. He has managed to establish himself as a successful landscaper, and he and his wife, Jane, have produced four beautiful daughters, who they encourage, protect, and love. As a child, Jon always laughed easily. Perhaps even then, he was able to see just how funny I really was.

42

So many of us go through life like this, and it can turn us into tyrants. Perhaps it's because we have a mean boss, and we have to go home and boss our spouses and children around to get even with life. Perhaps it's because as children we were told, "It's not worth doing if you can't do it right," and we took that to heart. Who knows? But it's no fun to live with someone who's always right, who always does everything perfectly, because that person is going to criticize just about anything family members do.

Can you let your husband load the dishwasher, even if you're having an anxiety attack about the stacking? Can you let your nine-year-old make the sandwiches for lunch, even if the mayonnaise dribbles down the sides of the bread? Can you let your wife take control of the remote for the evening? Can you let your children clean their rooms without redoing them? Do the toys really have to be put up in certain places? At work, can you go to the bathroom without worrying that people are going to come in and take your good pencils while you're gone?

Ta-Dah Number Two:
Talk to Yourself in Fun Ways

When we engage in positive self-talk—what I call "happy talk"—we reduce some of the stress in our lives. Words are not only descriptions, but prescriptions. They elicit emotional responses. They can be a cure or a curse.

It is important to take the time to develop a clear image of your goals and how you wish to achieve them. Consider all the barriers to your success, write them down, and say them out loud. Often just vocalizing the obstacles points out their absurdity. Ask your inner cheerleaders to help you out. Keep a copy of *The Little Engine That Could* handy. It's an excellent companion for positive thinking skills. By talking to ourselves in optimistic ways through positive affirmations, we can change how we feel by changing how we think.

It's a good idea to repeat affirmations to ourselves throughout the day. Here are eight steps to effective affirmations:

1. Make your affirmations short, clear, and specific. (For example, *I am good to my*

43

mother or *I turned in an excellent report at work.)*

2. Phrase them in the present tense. You want them to start taking effect today. *(I take a walk every morning.)*

3. Put them in very positive terms. *(I am a very caring person. I help others with kind words.)* Avoid words based on wish fulfillment, fear, or negativity.

44

4. Don't make affirmations about changing other people. Direct the attention toward changing yourself.

5. Write your affirmations when you're in a receptive state—after meditating or taking a nice long walk.

6. Keep your affirmations in handy places. Take them with you. Repeat them often. Keep in mind how long it took to create negative thoughts.

7. Change or rewrite your affirmations as you see fit. You may change your mind about a specific goal or need.

8. Have fun with your affirmations; don't make them a chore.

Here are some sample affirmations that you may want to use:

I am my own entertainment center.
As long as I show up, I'll have fun.
My body, mind, and spirit are joyful, happy, and energetic.
The child within embraces me.
For every obstacle there is a solution.
I am joyfully in the moment.
I enjoy others for who and for what they are.
I appreciate whatever is done for me.
I see the humor in myself.
I am free to express myself.
I play along the way.
I enjoy myself and others.
At work or at home I am healthy, happy, and fit.
I renew myself daily.
I support myself daily.
I support myself with kind, loving individuals.
I belly laugh as often as possible.
I am a cosmic joke.
I live in gratitude.
I laugh at myself, not at others.
I deserve pleasure.
Deadlines don't kill me.
I am able to say "I love you."
I give thanks often and out loud.
I stay open and available to new knowledge.
I realize I am not the center of the universe.

If you make it a practice to use daily affirmations, changing them as your life changes, the doom-and-gloom crowd in your head will soon retreat.

๏๏ ๏๏ ๏๏ ๏๏ ๏๏ ๏๏

Chapter 3

Awfulizing and Catastrophizing

Every other magazine I pick up has an article in it on how to increase the amount, quality, or intensity of your sex life. If the amount of information is comparable to the amount of sex people are engaging in, then emergency rooms across the nation must have standing room only.

I'm particularly fascinated by the statistics—or, more important, how they're compiled. I have never had anyone stop at my door and ask me how many times a week I have sex. Yet it appears that someone is doing just that. How else do they know that 5,000 individuals around the country were found to have sex twice a week, 3,000 do it once a week, 1,000 have it once every nine days, and 500 never do?

How does this happen? Does someone in a lab coat show up at your front door and proclaim,

"Hello. My name is Professor Seducto. I just happened to be in the neighborhood and I thought you might want to be a part of a weird little survey we're doing in your neck of the woods. It's going to appear in next month's *Newsweek*, but don't worry, your name won't be used."

My question is: Who cares? After I know about the rest of the world's sex life, what do I do? On top of everything else (no pun intended), I now can proceed to do a couple of things: Compare myself to the norm and make myself unhappy because I'm not up to par or discover I'm so above average that I may need a shrink because I have another addiction; or blame my spouse because I don't feel sexy, I don't act sexy, and when we do have sex, I'm not seeing fireworks. Or I can take the healthier route and laugh at the whole thing, because sex is supposed to be fun and not a job.

It appears, however, that what used to be considered an intimate and private part of life—something rather mysterious—is becoming as ordinary as advertisements on a box of Wheaties. I remember when I was 13, I loved books by Daphne du Maurier. *Frenchman's Creek* was a favorite. It was so romantic, and I recall how exciting it was when I got to the sexy part, which read, "He removed her earring." That was it— the rest was left to the imagination. Today he probably wouldn't remove her earring because more than likely he'd be wearing it.

In the movies and now even on television, not only does everything come off, but then the

48

camera zooms in and we get a close-up that could be used as a training video for gynecologists. It's a far cry from the time when Lucy and Desi Arnaz slept in twin beds with their pajamas and robes on, and had to keep one foot on the floor, even for a little peck on the cheek.

There is virtually nothing left to the imagination anymore, and I don't think this has been a good thing for most people's sex lives. Some of the sexual gymnastics would require lessons from Ringling Brothers. I wonder, *What is the goal?* If it's to resemble a human pretzel, then bravo. But how many of us have the flexibility, strength, and conditioning, or, more important, the need to replicate some of these improbable fantasies?

49

The movies and TV shows we watch spur comparisons, and we wind up resentful that our sex lives aren't like those on the big screen. Then we start to feel we've never really been sexy, we'll never have fun, we're too old already, and our lives are over. The bottom line is that most of us do not need to jump through hoops in our beds or go through the spin cycle with our mates to enjoy sex.

We're also surrounded by advertisements and commercials that tell us we need to be hot, hot, hot! That used to mean you needed a cool drink and a fan. Now if you're hot, you're sizzling, oozing with sexuality. Huge lips are in—the bigger the better, and breasts are lifted and drawn together in special bras left over from Conan the Barbarian's wardrobe.

Personally, I've never been able to figure out the hair thing. The sexy look involves hair flying all over the place. I'm assuming you're supposed to look like you just got out of bed after a lustful tryst. If that's the case, then I'm definitely missing out because when I'm in bed, my hair just gets flat.

In addition, there are incense, creams, mattresses that rock, videos that instruct, music to set the mood, and enough sexy lingerie to fill Madison Square Garden. Believe me, I've tried a lot of these things, and yes, they were fun and, on occasion, still are. However, things change—specifically, we change. I still have a drawer of sexy nighties, only my body has forgotten how to look in them.

50

There seems to be a lack of designers who create for Rubenesque shapes or, to be more specific, little avocados with legs. Perhaps as we age, we need to begin to enjoy each other for who and what we are, and not for who we think we need to be. I must admit that once in a while I am nostalgic for the way things were. But if passion and intensity in our sex lives is our primary goal, then we will never be rewarded with the enduring aspects of intimacy on a deeper level.

Occasionally I see an article or book that gives me pause, and I think, *I'm going to try this.* My latest experience was to try to create a more romantic setting by trying the latest 12-step program, "How to Increase the Love Life You Used to Have Before You Lost It." After sharing the 12 steps with my husband, I set a date for our romantic interlude. (In case you're not in the know, the best way to increase sex in your life is to schedule it. Experts in the area recommend writing it into your organizer. How spontaneous—now you have another job to do!)

The big day finally arrived. I cleaned the house, made a gourmet meal, brought in fresh flowers, burned the incense, and got a pink light bulb for the bedroom lamp. I also purchased about 50 candles to produce a soft glow. I slipped on the lacy lingerie, just in time to greet Bob as he walked in the door.

Bob looked like he'd had one of those days at the office. The one that means he needs to sit in his chair and stare. However, I steadfastly got him through dinner and into the bedroom. We slipped under the covers, but instead of starting with step number one, he went right to step five. I said, "What happened to two, three, and four? You really aren't giving me what I need!"

"Look," he said. "This is all I've got!"

Well, you can imagine the outcome. It definitely was not an uplifting experience. I got right into my blame game routine, and Bob got defensive. After a shout-and-pout ending, we both fell asleep, only to wake up to find the bedroom on fire. So much for 12 steps to sexiness. Give me my flannel nightgown and knee socks, and let the chips fall where they may.

51

Premeditated Suffering

Now, for some of us, an evening like that would lead to a whole day of awfulizing and catastrophizing. We'd be saying to ourselves, and to anyone else who'd listen: I'll never be beautiful. Things aren't good between us any more. I'm too old to enjoy life the way I used to. It's going to be a bad day.

These gloom-and-doom messages are what I call "premeditated suffering." It's when you can't enjoy the pleasure of anticipating an event because you're sure it's about to be ruined for you. For instance, I'll say to my husband, "Let's go to the movies." He'll say, "It's going to be crowded." I used to fight with him about this. Now I figure, hey, he's a prophet. I tell him, "You're amazing! You can see from here to the movies!"

People who awfulize say, "It's bad here. It's awful." And they want to predict more for later: "It's going to get much worse." If it's raining, we complain. Why can't we be like kids, who get up in the morning and can't wait to jump in the puddles? Instead we say, "I'm going to get wet."

Then you look in the mirror and start in on yourself: "How did this happen? I don't know how I got so heavy." When I used to teach aerobics, people would say, "I went to a wedding." I'd reply, "You got like this from one wedding?" Then they'd say they were bloated. So many people go around bloated, it's like we're a nation of walking waterbeds. So now it's raining, I'm bloated, and I'm so tired. Again, we need to learn from children. Have you ever heard a kid say, "I'm exhausted from playing. I think I need to lie down."

A woman named Sally, who attended one of my workshops, exemplified premeditated suffering perfectly. Sally told me she would warn her husband every morning before they left for work that she'd be exhausted when she got home that night. She wasn't content with just inflicting the suffering on herself; she wanted to spread it around so her husband couldn't enjoy the evening either. He knew from early on in the day that the night would be no fun. Yet Sally couldn't understand why her marriage broke up.

There are a frightening number of people like Sally in the world. To them, irrational behavior is no fun when it's practiced alone. They move in packs, using every opportunity to terrorize themselves and everyone they meet.

Take the nurse at one of the hospitals where I held a workshop. Whenever a patient was wheeled into the emergency room, she would exclaim, "Oh no, not another admission." Her colleagues would sigh in a show of sympathetic suffering. They didn't realize that without these patients, they'd be out of work, living under bridges instead of in comfortable suburban homes.

A lot of people like to say, "It's going to be a long day." Now, what *is* a long day? After all, how long can a day be? Every day has the same amount of hours; it's just your perception that changes it.

53

If you think you're going to suffer extensively that day, then sure, it's going to be long.

Every time I go to the mall with my friend Darlene, she announces, "We're not going to find any parking spaces." Darlene has decided that there aren't any to be found, so her attention naturally will focus on our not finding any. She'll drive past a space that the car would have fit into and say, "It was too small." Finally we'll wind up parking half a mile away from the entrance after driving around for 45 minutes, bypassing any number of possible parking spaces for various reasons (not enough room between cars; there's a puddle on the driver's side). In fact, Darlene isn't happy if we *do* find a parking space right away, because it upsets her vision of the world, which is essentially negative.

The same thing holds true, of course, once we make it into the mall. "I'll never find the right dress for my cousin's son's bar mitzvah." I'll ask what kind of outfit she's looking for, and she'll describe it to me in a vague way—"Oh, you know, something nice but not too dressy. Maybe with a jacket, kind of a suit thing." She does this because she knows I'm going to try to find the exact article of clothing that she describes, so she keeps it obscure on purpose. She doesn't *want* me to find the right dress for her, because then her negative predictions wouldn't work out as she'd planned. If she found the dress right off the bat, she couldn't bitch and moan through our whole lunch ("I knew

I wouldn't find it. They never have the right size for me. I've always had trouble fitting into dresses, the way they cut them").

Here's how to move from common sense to nonsense if you're into awfulizing:

1. Choose someone who's close to you, who is solidly based in reality. Someone who knows that when there's static on the TV, it doesn't mean that aliens are trying to take over the earth. Have a conversation with that person once a week and voice your concerns. Be open to his or her feedback. Try to stifle your "Yes, but they're probably coming to get me because I'm a vegetarian."

55

2. Record yourself talking on the phone. Play it back and start to listen to how you describe your life and the people in it. Are you drowning in self-pity? Is every situation a segment for *As the Stomach Turns?* Give yourself an Emmy for Best Dramatic Actor. Show it off to family and friends.

3. Get out the dictionary and look up words that have the ability to create fear and anxiety. Keep them handy, just in case you're at a loss for words. It may be time to really go over the edge with your awfulizing.

4. Give yourself permission to set aside 15 minutes a day for nothing but optimistic conversation. Say anything and everything that is riddled with hope and joy. If you can't think of anything to say, make it up. If you're going to have a hectic day, say to yourself, *I'm going to sail through this.* Eventually your mind won't know the difference.

5. Go all the way with it: Buy yourself a black cape with a hood and swoop around the house, commenting on how dangerous it is to take a bath, on how you might slip on the steps next winter when it snows, or on the fact that a meteorite is passing by the earth in the next millennium. Do what you do best, with great panache.

56

If You're Happy and You Know It . . .

Recently I was at the airport for a business trip, and my flight was canceled. Everyone was complaining and moaning. Finally we got a flight, and they were still upset. "It probably won't leave on time," I heard people saying. Then once they got on the plane, they complained about the size of the bins. "I need a bigger bin," I heard several people saying.

As I went down the aisle, I decided to liven things up. I said, "Hi, great to see you!" to three men sitting in one row. They all had a paper. Now, men don't like to get close. They were very uncomfortable sitting in this row. I said, "Isn't this exciting, look how close you are!" They just stared at me. Finally I got to my seat and started singing, "If you're happy and you know it . . ." I was pleased because everyone on the plane joined in. I lightened the load of a lot of people who'd have spent the whole time on the flight complaining, and all it took was a few silly comments and a little song.

And of course people awfulize about what's going to happen after they're dead. Joan Borysenko, whose brilliance is delightfully wedded to a great sense of humor, told me the following story:

Herbie and Mervin, two old guys, were sitting on a bench. They made a pact that the first one to die would come back and tell the other one what it was like. Well, Herbie dies, and about a month later Mervin is lying in his bed and he sees Herbie.

"My God, you came back!" Mervin says. "What's going on?"

Herbie says, "It ain't bad. I get up, eat breakfast, and have sex till noon. Then lunch, and sex till dinner. Then I have dinner, a little more sex, and I go to bed. I'm really content and satisfied."

Mervin says, "My God! Where are you?"

Herbie says, "I'm a bull in Colorado."

The best way to get past awfulizing is to think of our cup as being full—not half empty or half

57

full. As I said earlier, why would I want half a cup of anything, anyway? We need to come from a position of abundance rather than of scarcity. As Einstein said, "The universe is a friendly place."

This is not to say that bad things don't happen. We need to keep good judgment and practicality in the back of our minds. When you drive your car, you keep your jack in the trunk in case you have a flat. Pilots de-ice wings because a certain amount of worry is appropriate here. But this constant worry and awfulizing becomes inappropriate when you never enjoy the sunshine because you're sure clouds are going to come later on. Try to recognize and get rid of your catastrophizing and awfulizing, and your world will be a brighter place for it.

Ta-Dah Number Three:
Touch Someone Else's Life

Volunteering, sharing, or caring for a friend or family member not only lifts their spirits and yours, but it may even help you to be healthier. According to San Francisco researchers, acts of appreciation and caring actually can contribute to having a healthier heart. Doctors found that when we dwell on more altruistic actions, heart rates slow and levels of the disease-fighting chemical immunoglobulin A (igA) rise and stay that way for several hours. So many of our lives are cluttered with so much detail that we have forgotten that we are part and parcel of a larger community.

As I grew up in Brooklyn, my home was like Grand Central Station. People came and went, and some never left. No one was homeless back then; they all stayed with us. The characters that came and went are part of the tapestry of my life. They live on in many of the conversations my mother and I have now. No matter what time of day or night, there was food waiting and someone to share it with.

I have so many fond memories of my grandmother's chicken soup and her tiny meatballs in a hearty broth, which she was convinced could cure just about anything. There are thousands of individuals who have been the recipients of Francesca's healing foods. If anyone in the neighborhood was ill, the word went out and an entourage would immediately show up with baskets of food, words of cheer, and assurances that prayers would be said for a speedy recovery. Today you're lucky if you get one night in the hospital. You call a cab, go home and get into bed, and pray someone will find you if you drop dead before the coroner shows up.

Why not use a few hours here and there to give of yourself to others? Involve your children. It's one of the best ways to help them not to become "entitled." Stop in and welcome a new neighbor, pick up some flowers and leave them on a co-worker's desk, or pay the toll for the person in

59

back of you. The next time you're depressed, think about something you did that was kind and compassionate. Then enjoy the calmness these good feelings inspire.

෨ ෨ ෨   ෨ ෨ ෨

60

CHAPTER 4

IF YOU DON'T HAVE TO SUFFER, DON'T PRACTICE

It seems to me that the holidays are getting closer and closer together every year. The stores are decorated for Christmas by August, and the supermarket starts displaying fruitcakes and turkeys in September. Last Thanksgiving, I actually got time off for good behavior. After 35 years of stuffing the bird, I got the opportunity to stuff myself at a local restaurant. I was waited on, someone else got to scrub the pans, and there was no endless wrapping of leftovers.

This year, however, it was back to the same old same old. The gang, which includes 3 children, 11 grandchildren, my mother, etc., stayed for five days. I don't know about anyone else's family, but our gathering is similar to an Italian opera: lots of high drama with a comic flavor. My mother, who took lessons from Don Corleone in *The Godfather*, begins her doom-and-gloom phone calls about two months prior to the event. "Where are you going to put everyone? What are we going to eat? Make sure you buy enough—the stores will be out of everything by the week of Thanksgiving. I hate the holidays! Maybe I just won't come."

This last statement is supposed to evoke heavy begging on my part. My standard response is "Oh please come, it wouldn't be the same without you." Sound familiar to any of you?

Once that scene was played, we got to the next act, which is the decision about what to eat. The phone calls from my mother and children increased as the holiday drew near. One's on this diet, one doesn't eat meat. My shopping list expanded to notebook length; I think I bought six different kinds of milk. All this was further complicated by the fact that my son Erik, who has studied the culinary arts, expects me to provide only the finest ingredients and utensils. He's like the temperamental chef in the movie *Big Night:* only the best, no compromises. It's a good thing his wife, Dawn, finds it amusing, or I might find him sitting on my steps surrounded by his pots and pans.

The last time Erik came for the holidays, he arrived with a new set of knives in a leather briefcase. He couldn't get over how I could keep on using my deformed cutlery. Of course, before he took cooking classes, he wolfed down my meals for 18 years without complaint.

When everyone came, the refrigerator was stocked. I had extra mattresses, blankets, and a new

62

set of knives. I was ready. But did I enjoy myself? At times, when I wasn't scraping pans or stirring sauces, I certainly did. But could I have had a lot more time to spend with my family—which, after all, is supposed to be the point of getting together for the holidays—if I hadn't caved in to all the requests like a classic martyr? If I'd said, "I'm cooking one meal, and then we're either going out for the rest or you guys will take turns cooking," that would have been a lot more fair, and I'd have had a lot more time to play with my grandkids, who don't have such elaborate gourmand tastes.

Remember that no one in your family really wants to watch you struggle or listen to you complain. It makes them feel guilty, and it just isn't fun. But if you're into your familiar role of being the martyr, you'll want that more than you want the help. I often joke that someone could make a lot of money selling a martyr kit: You put a piece of Velcro around your forehead and a piece around your wrist. Slap them together, and you can walk around moaning, looking just like my grandmother Francesca.

63

Super Mom or Super Tired?

Do you feel that you're consistently taken advantage of? That you deserve nothing and need nothing? When someone asks you what's wrong, do you answer, "If you loved me, you'd know"? If so, then your brand of stinking thinking is making you a martyr.

You're so good, so decent. You won't get your reward until you get to heaven. This kind of thinking ran in my family, particularly with Francesca. A lot of times the women in the family tend to fall into this trap. We always had a lot to do at home, but now many of us have careers on top of it. Nowadays we call them "Super Moms"—but are you actually Super Mom, or just Super Tired?

During the day, Super Mom is dressed in a pinstriped suit, white blouse, and smart black pumps. She carries an attaché case and walks with an air of confidence. Before work, at night, and on the weekends, this same woman becomes a wife, mother, chauffeur, exercise enthusiast, shopper, cook, cleaner, volunteer worker, and, last but not least, a sex goddess. If that description alone left you exhausted, then you can understand how millions of women feel every day. Liberation arrived in the 1970s, making it possible for women to have to do everything they did before in the home, plus have a demanding career on top of it.

The workshops on assertiveness say: "Delegate responsibility. Learn to relax. Let some things go." Now, I believe it's easier to delegate a job at work than it is at home. If you don't think this is true, just ask your kids to clean the bathroom and watch them get instant flu. Somehow it seems impossible to train the family to use the washer, dryer, and dishwasher. Folding laundry was a five-week

64

intensive course at my house. Learning how to change the vacuum bag took six months. Bathroom cleaning was a yearlong project. I decided to divide the kitchen into sections, starting with the sink.

Of course, you can try to do it all, or you can learn to give some of it up. The people who won't give it up are getting off on being a martyr. They're into doing it all, but they make their families miserable by their constant moaning and groaning about how much they're doing. They tend to be perfectionists, too, so no one can do it like they can—they have to be the ones to do the laundry and take out the garbage. This attitude builds into a classic case of martyrdom that would make Joan of Arc look like she had nothing to complain about.

Guilt also contributes to martyrdom, since many of us feel undeserving when life treats us well. Some analysts agree that the most powerful guilt results from competing with and surpassing our parents. Women fear outstripping their mothers, and men fear outdoing their fathers. It feels like a form of betrayal. I like to call guilt "the gift that keeps on giving," because it is self-perpetuating. Once you get into a guilt syndrome, it's hard to get out of it, and it's going to contribute to your martyr mind-set. (Let's not forget that guilt has its uses. For instance, guilt provides us with a conscience. Holding up a 7-Eleven *should* make us feel guilty.)

There are martyrs at work, too. Are you the one who always gets in at 7 A.M. and never leaves the office until after 7 P.M.? Do you make a point of announcing every morning how late you stayed the night before? Do you secretly enjoy the fact that you're the only person in your office who knows all the housekeeping personnel by name? Do you constantly volunteer for huge projects that add on to your normal workload—and then complain about it? If so, you're a martyr at work, and your colleagues are probably sick of hearing you go on and on about it.

I often wonder why more people don't use humor in their professional lives. Humor is such a great icebreaker, and a good motivator, too. But people want to cling to their roles as martyrs. It's hard to be perceived as a workhorse if you're not afraid to be funny in the workplace. Yet there are a lot of ways to use humor at work without appearing unprofessional. After all, if you have your D.D.S., your M.D., your S.D., your R.N., and your P.D.Q., you certainly don't want to blow it by seeming unprofessional! (I have a D.M.A.—Don't Mean Anything!) When you die, people will remember that you shared some joy, that you made life more comfortable for them, instead of remembering your degrees. Did you ever see a tombstone with a degree on it?

Use of humor won't make you look bad, but acting like a martyr on the job will. Leo Buscaglia used to go up to people and say, "How do you feel?" The person would respond, "Fine." He'd say, "Why don't you tell your face?" Think of the comments you make at work. People say things like: "I don't feel too good. I have a backache, my stomach

66

hurts, my shoulder blades are stiff. And I haven't peed all day!"

Why do I want this information? Why do I want to know that I'm working with someone who hasn't peed all day? Instead, people should come up and say, "I went, I went, I'm totally empty!" What if someone came up to you at the office and said, "I feel great! I can't believe it, I'm off the charts!" People would look at her and think, *Oh my God, she's on drugs!* We're not expected to feel great, particularly if we're into our martyr behavior.

If you're acting like a martyr, you need to be honest with yourself. Do you always want to be exhausted, the wet blanket on all the fun? A martyr dampens the spirits of any office, social group, or family. What child can enjoy himself when Mom and Dad are always complaining that they're tired from all they're doing? My mother used to come home and tell me she'd worked like a dog. What does that mean, anyway? And she'd add that she was doing all this for me. Martyrdom often comes with strings attached.

67

Today's woman is trying to juggle an enormous number of tasks in her quest for a fulfilling life. Women's inherent nature is to nurture. Therefore, it's difficult to give up tasks we feel are native to us. However, particularly if we assume the role of breadwinner as well as mom and housekeeper, we must realize that others in the family can chip in and help. Or, God forbid, we can hire help if we can afford it.

Children can do many things to help out, even at an early age, if they are taught. A child of three can pick up her toys and put them in her toy box. A child of nine can load the dishwasher. Husbands can help, too, but remember that often you have to ask. A lot of women are too proud to ask for help, thinking, *If he loved me, he'd help out.* But often this doesn't work with men. They're great if a specific problem is pointed out and you ask for help with it, but don't expect a lot of men to notice the sink is filthy or the garbage needs taking out. Yet you may be amazed at what your spouse will do if you merely ask.

As my Thanksgiving story illustrates, martyrdom often makes its appearance during holidays. Even if your version of cooking most of the year is to put the microwave timer on "5 minutes," somehow on holidays it seems that women feel they have to cook. Even if they stayed at the office until nine the night before Thanksgiving, they're still going to have to have that turkey with his mom's recipe for homemade pork stuffing, even if they have to stay up all hours to create it.

The following are some ways for martyrs to move from common sense to nonsense:

1. Learn to use the word *no.* A lot of martyrdom is based on the misguided notion that others won't be able to survive without us. Even though we are on the verge of exhaustion, we continue to provide

support. The more we do, the more we resent those we are doing for. Underneath it all is an overwhelming need for approval, which we never seem to get. After years of our being the doormat, people find it hard to stop wiping their feet on us.

There are some things you can choose not to do. If "no" feels uncomfortable, say, "Let me think about that." This gives you the opportunity not to plunge in right away.

2. Decide what types of things you need to do for yourself. Taking care of yourself helps keep you from falling apart. When's the last time you soaked in a hot tub without feeling guilty for taking a few extra minutes for yourself? Put time for yourself into your daily planner so you've made an appointment with yourself to walk, daydream, or pursue your hobbies.

3. Inform your family that you are taking certain times out of the week to self-nurture. They may balk at first, but ultimately, they will have more respect for you. People tend to take advantage of those who give no boundaries or limits. It's also a healthier role model for your

children, particularly for young girls. It has been found that when mothers are prone to martyrdom, their daughters will begin to emulate them in early adolescence, leading to problems of low self-esteem.

4. Create a chart with chores for everyone in your family. If you live alone, try to find outside help. If that seems unaffordable, you may be able to barter. Allowing others to help you is an act of giving. It says, "I trust you and believe in your abilities." When we have to do it all ourselves, we're actually taking away others' capacity to become responsible.

70

5. Of course, you always can go to the other extreme and use your martyrdom to get what you need. Pump it up, wear a tiara, and carry a wand. Wherever you go, tell everyone what you did for them today and how good you were to do it. Tell them you're thinking of erecting a monument in your backyard or office that has your name in bold letters, with Too Good to Be True under it. Remember that when you turn martyrdom into mayhem, it becomes comical. Ethel Barrymore once said, "The first day you laugh at yourself, you grow up."

Men Are Martyrs, Too

Of course, men can be martyrs, too. I don't think there's a woman alive who experiences a cold, bad back, or a stubbed toe quite like a man. They won't say anything at work because it would be a sign of weakness, but just wait until they get in the door or, God forbid, they take a few days off. The only way you will escape the pity party is if you're off to work yourself. Then you'll only get the end-of-the-day report on how many boxes of tissues were used and how exhausting the nose-blowing was.

If you happen to be home during the day, forget about having any time to yourself. You have now been designated head nurse of the intensive care unit. Sterilize everything, line up the aspirin, get the cauldron of chicken soup ready, and tape the number of your local paramedics to your telephone. You are on emergency status.

Whenever my husband gets sick, he uses the word *honey* a lot. Periodically I'll hear his frail voice emanating from the bedroom: "Honey, honey, I need some juice, could you get me a little juice, honey?" I get the juice, a few minutes pass, and the voice starts again. "Honey, honey, feel my head. Do you think I have a temperature?" After several honey, honeys, I start to get a twisted look on my face. I tell him that several cases of bubonic plague have been reported in the neighborhood. I say that health officials suspect it began in our backyard

71

with a huge infestation of gigantic mosquitoes that are attracted to tall men with white hair named Bob. My humor is looked upon with great distaste, and I'm accused of being uncaring and hostile. Ah, the insights we get when we're sick.

There also needs to be a lot of quiet. Each time the phone rings, it's accompanied by "Who is that? Don't they know I'm sick?" I suggested that he give me more notice the next time he thinks he's getting sick, so I can call *PrimeTime Live* and have them do a special on it. They could make an announcement that under no circumstances should anyone call the LaRoche household during this time of duress. I also suggested that the next time he feels a cold coming on, he might want to sign up for a retreat at a monastery. Then the only sounds he'd hear would be the monks praying for him.

When I have a cold, somehow or other I manage to function at home and at work, like most other women. And it's not because we're any better. It's because we're trained from the time we have children to get up 30 times a night to take care of them, even though we may be in a full-body cast. In addition, no man has had to deal with a monthly cycle when you feel like you need a blood transfusion and your body feels like a giant mushroom gone mad.

Believe me, I'm not trying to see who can win the martyr crown, but how about a little equanimity here? The next time I'm trying to breathe out of completely clogged nostrils and I'm hacking away, somebody please get me a glass of water because I'm sure my husband will be watching a program he can't leave until the commercial comes on. Unless he's sick, too, and then while I'm gasping my last breath I'll hear, "Honey, honey . . ."

Ta-Dah Number Four:
Take Time to Listen to Yourself

Meditation shows us the possibility of listening to our inner voice, and one of the great researchers on the benefits of meditation is Dr. Herbert Benson. His book *The Relaxation Response* has become a classic. There are two basic components involved in eliciting the relaxation response. The first is using a mental focus, such as watching your breath; repeating a word, phrase, prayer, or sound; or using repetitive muscular activity to help you shift your mind from everyday thoughts and worries. The second is having a passive attitude toward distracting thoughts. Don't worry about how well you are doing, but gently direct your mind back to your mental or exercise focus when you notice yourself caught up in a train of thought.

Here are the basic steps necessary to elicit the relaxation response:

Pick a focus word, phrase, image, or prayer. This can be rooted in your personal belief system; for example, a Christian might choose the opening of Psalm 23, "The Lord is my shepherd"; a Jew,

73

"Shalom"; and a Muslim, "Allah." Or you may prefer a neutral word or phrase, such as "peace" or "love."

You also may choose to focus on your breathing. Sit quietly in a comfortable position, close your eyes, relax your muscles, and breathe slowly and naturally. As you do, repeat your focus word or phrase as you exhale. Assume a passive attitude. Don't worry about how well you are doing. When other thoughts come to mind, simply say to yourself, *Oh, well,* and gently return to the repetition. Continue for 10 to 20 minutes, and practice once or twice daily.

74

CHAPTER 5

DON'T "SHOULD" ON YOURSELF

L ast week I spent more than six hours doing a seminar standing in a pair of black high-heeled pumps. During the day, I was in varying states of discomfort. It's more truthful to say I was in searing white-hot pain that began at my feet and proceeded to the base of my brain. When I finally had the opportunity to remove my shoes and get relief, I realized my feet had been permanently molded into triangles.

After my experience with the cruel shoes, I decided to check out some of the other shoe styles to see if I could find a pair that were comfortable— in other words, something designed for the human foot. What I found were more pumps with points, flats with points, and sneakers. Since I didn't want to repeat my episode of torture, I chose to return to an outdated pair of shoes with round toes. I may sound like a heretic to those who faithfully follow the dictates of fashion, but I'm no longer willing to trade glamour for pain.

Pain involves a great deal of stress. In all the reams of literature written on stress, there is nothing that addresses clothing or personal grooming aids as being stressful. Yet I'm sure many of you have fallen victim to buying fashions, products, or gadgets to enhance your looks that ended up being expensive, stressful experiences.

The following are some cruel items that I've done battle with:

— **Jeans:** If anyone has discovered a pair that fits a short woman with a small waist, ample hips, and short legs, please let me know. I've given up. If they fit my waist, they're too tight in the hips. When the hips fit, the waist bags out, which makes me look like an inverted avocado. Even the companies that make petite jeans still make the legs too long.

— **Panty hose:** I've had many a fit over these. Ever try to put them on in a hurry? The front looks like the back, and vice versa. If you have any rough edges on your fingernails, forget it. Never, ever believe the size chart, unless you plan to commit suicide. If they say petite, they mean toddler. I have gotten them halfway up my hips and found there was no more material for the rest of the way. Pulling and tugging gets you nothing but a hole. When

they're too big, you spend your day tactfully trying to pull them up. One solution is to always have
three pairs on hand: one to experiment with, one to
cut up to get even, and the other to wear.

Also on my stress list are gels that stiffen your
hair so you need a hammer and chisel to remove
them, deodorant that burns your armpits, lipstick
that comes off on everything, mascara that won't
come off unless you detach your eyelashes, zippers
that have too much material under them so they
get stuck halfway (the only solution is a demoli-
tion team), and coats that get in the way of driving
the car.

Also on my list are bras that are for people
with banana-shaped breasts, underpants that fit so
tightly around your thighs they stop the circula-
tion, and, last but not least, manufacturers who
make clothing that says "medium" and "large,"
but which you know in your soul is a small. These
people deserve to wear my cruel black shoes every
day for a week—with panty hose, naturally.

Now, why do we put ourselves through these
stressful grooming and dressing experiences? Why
do we tell ourselves we "should" fit into a smaller
size; we "should" wear fashionable, painful shoes
so we'll look smart; and we "should" lose weight
so we'll look fashionably thin?

Many people never miss a chance to lay a
"should" or "shouldn't" on themselves, their character, their appearance, and what they think, feel,

77

say, or do. Are you always "shoulding" on yourself? To the outside world, this makes you appear very conscientious, but it also reminds you that you're not quite right just as you are. It's a subtle but extremely effective way to ensure your continuing low self-esteem, which is probably the number one misery maker in the universe.

You have assumed that you're a problem and that you always will be unless you constantly nag at yourself. You criticize and "should" on yourself when anything bad happens. You think of things that you could have done to change the scenario, "if only" you'd done them. You didn't, so you're to blame.

78

If you "should" on yourself a lot, you probably "should" on others as well. As always, misery loves company. You move from discussing with friends, family, and significant others the things *you* should have done differently in your life to the things *they* should have done differently. There's a natural progression from one to the other.

Often your "shoulds" depend on someone else's judgment. If you can't meet that person's expectations or those of society in general, you've failed. You feel inadequate and incompetent; you feel like a loser.

The truth is, after all these "shoulds"—I should have lost weight, should have gotten up earlier, should have finished that project over the week-end—you're so down from berating yourself that you don't have the energy to enjoy life. All the energy we spend on our "shoulds" could be used to do something productive, including relaxing.

I'm Not Afraid of Heights, Just Widths

My big "should" in life has always been associated with my weight. I've finally realized that trying to be thin is at odds with my Sicilian roots. When I was a child, food was fun, it was security, and it was an expression of love. My grandmother Francesca stood at the stove, stirring, tasting, and directing my grandfather to bring her ingredients. Her sauce sat on the stove simmering for hours, steam rising like a dormant volcano. The odor permeated the house, creeping into every crevice and lingering long after the sauce was eaten.

79

Food also created a sense of community when I was growing up. Neighborhood women filled our kitchen, comparing favorite recipes in the hopes of outdoing each other. They helped create a feeling of abundance in the midst of scarce resources. Now an Act of Contrition accompanies every morsel that goes into our mouths.

In contrast, when I was a child, someone was always chanting, "Eat, eat, you need to eat." Being too thin was sacrilegious. Women were expected to be round. If you resembled a sausage with legs, you were considered beautiful. If your collar, hip, or ankle bones were too prominent, you were compared to a chicken. Francesca conducted a pinch test to see if you were getting too thin. If she felt too little flesh, she immediately took your temperature and upped your spaghetti quotient.

I remember how horrified my grandmother was after I had my first child. I had slimmed down to the proportions of a hot, sexy babe. Francesca took one look and said, "You like this diet. Don't worry, you're going to die soon, and you'll be the thinnest one in the cemetery." Her rebuke was a prophecy. I didn't die, but like millions of other women, I have tortured myself in the name of being the thinnest female in town.

I became obsessed with thinness quite innocently. It started at one of the first coffee klatches I went to. For those under 50, a coffee klatch was a precursor of the *Oprah* show. Women in the neighborhood got together and discussed everything, revealed everything. The hot topics were always sales at Abraham & Straus, Macy's, or Gimbels and who was on a diet. Some women devoted their entire conversation to their quest for lettuce that tasted like lasagna. My friends exercised, counted calories, and attended diet seminars. Some commented on how wonderful it felt to feel hungry. Since I had never felt hungry, this seemed to be a ridiculous attitude. Initially I coped by repeating my grandmother's prophecy. This fell on deaf ears. It took me a while to become a full-fledged member of the diet cult, but eventually I converted.

Every dieter has her moment of truth. Mine came when I went shopping for a bathing suit.

I decided to be daring and try on a two-piece.
Up until then, I had worn the orthopedic variety
appropriate for a mother. But since bikinis were
in, I thought, *Why not?* Why not, indeed. What
the sales clerk handed me looked like a blindfold
for a gerbil. When I gazed into the mirror, what
I saw was, to say the least, unappealing. In fact, I
was in shock.

And so, in that year of our Lord 1965, I created
my mission statement: I will diet! I will exercise! I
will be thin! I tried the Stillman Diet, which meant
18 glasses of water a day, lots of meat, and a constant search for a bathroom. Other diets soon followed. The Atkins Diet—lots of fat and bad breath.
And the Sprout Diet, which is great if you're a goat.
All failed.

81

I moved on to more organized efforts: Weight
Watchers, the Diet Center, Nutri/System, and
Optifast. Since none worked, I joined a gym. I
found one close to home that was run by a woman
who looked like Arnold Schwarzenegger in drag.
She put me through a program that would cause
a marine to fall to his knees. I persevered. I would
not wimp out, I vowed. My mission was to reach
34-24-34 and take no prisoners.

After the first day at the gym, I was in severe
pain, but I was happy because I felt I was one of
the guys. I could pump iron with the best of them.
As I continued my workouts, I became intent upon
reducing my thighs. I measured them every day.
My mood matched the results. My family always

knew when my thighs refused to respond to my efforts. My children would pass along the word: "Stay away. Mom's having a bad thigh day."

I soon heard of a doctor who dispensed "magic" pills. Like thousands of other women at that time, I got these pills and followed Dr. Anorexia's instructions: "Two pills every day. See me in two weeks for your next supply. And please write me a check toward my Caribbean vacation."

The pills worked, in a manner of speaking. I got thin rapidly because I couldn't stop moving. I was a whirling dervish. I had the most immaculate house in the neighborhood. The local hospital called, wanting to use my kitchen as an operating room. After three months of seeing Dr. Anorexia, I was so wired I could have been an electrical outlet for a chain saw.

But after a while, things started to reverse themselves. When you can't think or sleep and you're having anxiety attacks, what do you do? You eat to calm yourself down, your metabolism slows down, and, you guessed it . . . you gain weight.

What happened next? I joined the aerobic revolution, a fancy word for jumping up and down. I jumped. I low-impacted. I high-impacted. People around me got thin; I got shin splints and my breasts got a foot longer.

Then it was on to everything New Age. I became a vegetarian and voraciously ate pounds of legumes (commonly known as beans). Fiber was in, and the resulting by-product had the power to send a Patriot missile to any part of the world. I began to resemble a zeppelin. When I started to salivate whenever I went by a McDonald's, I knew it was time to banish the beans.

When I reached 49, panic set in. It had been over 20 years since I had made it my goal to be slim and trim. I had no medals, no certificates to show for my years of trial and error—only a lot of stretch marks. Just when I thought I would self-destruct on a 12-piece Colonel Sanders chicken pack and an ice-cream cake from Carvel, I saw a magazine article about how low-fat eating was the answer to weight loss. At that moment, I had an epiphany. I became a low-fat spiritualist.

Unfortunately, counting fat grams is about as much fun as being frigid. Nonetheless, it became a national pastime, and I didn't want to be left out. I finally realized I had hit the wall when I went to a restaurant and ate the centerpiece, a candle, and a plastic banana.

I'm glad to report that I finally get it. I'm stuck with parts of me, like terminal saddlebags. All those years of trying to get rid of the cellulite on the back of my thighs, but then I finally realized I'd never have anyone that short following me!

Eating healthily, exercising moderately, and especially enjoying food are the keys to a happy life. I have come full circle to my grandmother's secret for a long life. She lived to 93, and was robust and healthy. The wooden spoon in her hand was a tribute to love, laughter, and lots of lasagna.

All this is to say that I wasted too many years "shoulding" on myself—I should lose weight, I should be thin, I should exercise—when I could have been enjoying my food and relaxing about my weight. All that time and money I wasted, trying to be a body size I could never attain in a million years. This is what happens when you "should" on yourself.

Instead, we need to realize that we're not perfect. We are probably never going to look like the models in those magazines. It's important to realize that you don't have to conform to anyone's ideals for looks or clean-house standards or work methods. You're the one who sets the goals and who decides what's necessary in your own life, and no one else. Don't let anyone (including those in media and advertising) impose their vision of beauty or success upon you. If you can relax and stop "shoulding" on yourself, you're going to enjoy life much more.

Here are some steps to move from common sense to nonsense when we "should" on ourselves:

84

1. Whenever you get caught up in thinking about what you should have done, stop and think about what a waste of energy that is. You can't go back and do it, because that period of time has passed. As long as you're still breathing, there's a possibility that you can

do it now. However, if you have no intention to follow through, give it up and move on.

2. Buy yourself a whip and keep it handy. Every time you start to drown yourself or others in "shoulds," grab the whip and give yourself a good beating. You're already self-flagellating, so why not do it as authentically as possible?

3. Keep a "should" journal. You'll probably be shocked to discover how many times a day "shoulda, coulda, woulda" comes out of your mouth.

4. There are certain chores in life that have to be done. Do them to the best of your ability and then forget about them.

5. Don't allow "shoulding" to go on at home or at work. Ask people to express themselves in better ways. "Shoulding" is filled with judging and finding fault. As a result, our surroundings become a courtroom filled with prosecutors and defense attorneys. Keep in mind that there are always exceptions and special circumstances that can change how things are supposed to be.

Chew It, Swallow It, Love It

Food has almost become poison in our society. We never come home to great smells simmering on the stove anymore. What's going to smell in the microwave? A great book on the topic of the whole concept of enjoyment is *Healthy Pleasures* by David Sobel. In it he discusses the idea that food should be fun. After all, we have to eat to nourish ourselves; therefore, we ought to feel good about the act of eating.

Here's something to try: When you put food into your mouth—whatever it is you choose to eat—chew it, swallow it, and love it! We don't do that anymore. As we're eating, we're thinking, *I don't know if I should have eaten that.* Then we ask two or three other people, "Do you think I should have eaten this? Have you eaten it before? What did it do to you? I bet I'm going to get fat from this. Everything I eat makes me fat. Oh God, I'm going to get bloated."

Anytime you eat something, someone reports to you what's in it. There's always some fat-gram police around, whether it's on the box or can label, or your girlfriend who's got it all memorized. "How many grams do you think are in this? Have you reached your quota for today?" We're eating low fat, so we'll live a long time, as miserably as possible!

And why is it that although we are so aware of fat grams, as a nation we're getting fatter? I know

86

why: "Low fat" is a misnomer. People think they can eat the entire box if it's low fat. But if you simply ate moderate amounts of all kinds of foods—everything you liked—you'd probably be a normal size. However, our mentality seems to be that we want to overeat, and then we want the one big diet that's a cure-all. As I said, I've gained and lost a tribe of people on all these diets. Once you make food the enemy, you have a problem. We need to start enjoying what we eat. Find a weight that's reasonable, and carry on with your life.

Think of things that you used to eat as a child or things that you've eaten lately that tasted just marvelous. When you ate these things, you simply glowed. Now eat at least two of these foods every week and enjoy the experience. Don't let yourself feel any guilt over it, and don't let yourself "should" over it. Just eat and enjoy. You can even start a food journal, listing the great things you ate that day. If you ate something scrumptious, write it down. Then go back and review your notes at the end of the week and enjoy the memories.

87

Diary of a Makeover Junkie

Not only do we "should" on our weight, but we "should" on our faces, skin, and hair, too. Most of us spend a fortune on products that are supposed to make us look good. On average, every woman uses 21 products each day in order to appear "natural."

Every spring I experience the desire for a metamorphosis, an impulse caused only partially by the change in seasons. Women's magazines are the real culprits, as they normally trumpet the mystical powers of the makeover as the cure for most of life's problems. Like many women, after spending the winter indoors, underexercised, and overfed—with my skin turning almost reptilian from the dry heat—I annually pursue a "new look." I race to the drugstore, scoop up as many magazines as I can carry, and head home, determined to get this over with as soon as possible.

Last spring I lucked out. The first article I stumbled upon was entitled "Do You Need a Makeover?" It asked a series of questions about makeup, skin care, weight, clothing, and personality. It then discussed each body part and provided simple suggestions for change at a minimal cost.

When I added up my score, my look was in the "uncomely weasel" range. My skin was too dry in some areas and too oily in others. And I had large pores. In fact, I was the Pavarotti of pores, a disaster for someone like me who often appears in public. Imagine lecturing while audience members shield their eyes as the television lights bounce off my craterlike pores. Soon I'd have to make my appearances veiled like a Middle Eastern matron.

I had more problems. My makeup was definitely old fashioned, somewhere between ancient Greece and Native American. I was not contouring my eyes properly. So I spent 30 minutes putting on makeup to make my eyes look bigger. (As if someone were going to come over and say, "I've noticed they're a millimeter larger today!") And my measurements were off, too—I would have to start my thin-thighs program again, and immediately. Unfortunately, no thin-arm program accompanied the thigh transformation routine.

However, I scored very high in personality. My mother must have taken this test for me when I was a child, because I remember her saying, "Don't worry about the rest of it; you have a great personality." I wonder if Cindy Crawford's mom told her the same thing.

Why do we all feel we need to be six feet tall and have stunning long blond hair, perfect teeth, and a fabulous figure? How about five foot one, solid build, dark hair, with the ability to dig up a garden and plant it? Or five foot five, long nose and no breasts, brilliant at numbers, and at the top of her profession? Maybe we think it's not fair that we aren't taller, thinner, more beautiful. Well, that's not important in the grand scheme of things. Give me some real finesse, like keeping a smile on your face while the toilet overflows, the vacuum cleaner sucks up your wedding band, and your son totals the car.

How about a prize for not having a nervous breakdown because you have a full-time job in addition to running the house? What about an award for preparing a fabulous dinner for your boss and her husband, only to watch your cat barf on the rug just as they're walking up the sidewalk? As far as verbal skills, I know plenty of people, like myself, who've had to cope with teenagers whom they've just told to come home by 11 P.M.

I think it's time for us average-looking-but-extraordinarily-likable people to realize we don't need to have a makeover every spring or to participate in anyone's beauty contest. We're beautiful every day, especially on the inside. So the next time you start to "should" on your weight, your looks, or your lack of exercise, try to keep this in mind.

90

Ta-Dah Number Five:
Treat Yourself to Pleasure and Passion

Why is it so difficult to enjoy ourselves without feeling guilty? Like my grandfather's prescription for wine and spaghetti, at times you have to let yourself go and "just enjoy."

In a study of 96 volunteers, Arthur Stone, Ph.D., a psychologist from the State University of New York, found that pleasant events such as dinner with friends or a weekend hike in the woods gave a boost to the immune system that lasted for two to three days. In contrast, a stressful encounter such as an argument with a boss or spouse had a lesser effect, slightly depressing the immune system for just one day. It appears that the absence of ordinary pleasures may take an even greater toll on our health than stress does.

Remember that pleasure can go from the sublime to the ridiculous, from simple to sumptuous, and from free to expensive. It isn't our budget that limits us but our minds. Have a real ice-cream cone with sprinkles or, God forbid, a hot fudge sundae. Take a garden tour or a hot air balloon ride, go for a manicure or ask a friend to give you one. Or go to two movies in one day.

One of my favorite pleasures is waking up early and sitting in my cozy chair while I sip a hot cup of coffee. The aroma, the chair, the beginning of the day are all simple luxuries. Working in my garden is deeply rewarding, especially when I have the whole day to weed, clip, and haul dirt. Being out in nature takes me away from my worry department. I feel pleasantly fatigued, and none of the birds ever asks me to make it lunch.

One of my ultimate sources of pleasure is making fresh spaghetti sauce from scratch, cooking some spaghetti, and sitting down to the fabulous results—liberally sprinkled with Parmesan, of course. I feel connected to my roots, nurtured and content; I feel proud to continue the tradition of love, laughter, and spaghetti.

No matter what time of day or night, my grandmother would be willing, ready, and able to make what she called her Little Red Sauce. I hope you'll try it and savor not only the aroma but the love that goes with it.

91

Francesca's Little Red Sauce

¼ cup olive oil

Fresh basil

1 small onion, chopped

Dash of oregano

5 cloves garlic, minced

Salt and pepper to taste

2 pounds plum tomatoes, blanched, skinned, and chopped or one 28-ounce can plum tomatoes

1 pound pasta, cooked

Freshly grated Parmesan cheese

Heat the oil in a saucepan and simmer the onion and garlic. Throw in the tomatoes and raise the heat until it starts to bubble. Add the basil, oregano, salt, and pepper. Break up the tomatoes with a fork and stir the sauce occasionally.

Cook about 20 minutes and pour over the pasta. Sprinkle with freshly grated Parmesan cheese. *Mangia!*

৩৩ ৩৩ ৩৩   ৩৩ ৩৩ ৩৩

CHAPTER 6

WORRYWARTS

In my most recent pilgrimage to the local book-store, I was drawn to a section with the heading "Latest Books on Anti-aging." My first response was that if I don't age, then I'll die. But that type of thinking has too much common sense attached to it. The latest American fetish is the discussion and promotion of books and products that halt or diminish the ravages of getting older. There are pills, potions, and procedures to smooth, tighten, and lift ancient parts that are winding down like an old clock.

Ironically, much of the scientific research is done on mice, which don't live very long anyway. Are we to believe that a human being isn't much more than a big mouse? I personally have never seen a wrinkled mouse. None of the nursing homes I've been in has had mice hanging around in the halls.

The dilemma seems to be about what to take, how much, and when. Do I take melatonin to sleep better, even though it might give me nightmares? Do I take DHEA hormone to increase my libido, even though it could make me grow facial hair? Now I'm feeling sexy, but I have to shave my mustache. How many vitamins do I take, in what order, and how will my body know what to do with them? Perhaps worrying about it all creates the most aging.

I must admit that I've had my share of fears and tears about the advancing years, but you really have to laugh at what's going on. Anytime I have a concern about getting older, I immediately call my 96-year-old mother to hear one of her uplifting messages. "You think that's bad? You haven't seen anything yet!" This always makes me feel grateful for a few days. Then I get sucked back in again, particularly after watching a 60-year-old movie star say she's never had any nips or tucks, and that what you see is merely the result of years of natural living and eating. How natural is it to have your eyebrows meet your hair? Should your face look like you just stepped out of a wind tunnel?

Magazines are loaded with ads showing underwear that is supposed to lift and firm, most of which was designed by sadists. I remember my grandmother's undergarments, which at the time I thought I'd never be caught dead in. Now I realize she was simply a sensible woman in tune with the aging process. Her bra was very sturdy; the straps were wide enough to hold up the Brooklyn Bridge. She used to wear big pink bloomers with plenty of room in them. I remember them hanging on the line like huge flags blowing in the breeze.

Nowadays, no matter what size underwear comes in, it looks like it's made for toddlers. The thongs really get me. I don't think anyone should be wearing those. Why are we paying for a strip of material that gives you a wedgie? We spend the first part of our lives trying to get rid of wedgies and the second part putting them back! Men seem to be a little more sensible in this area. They wear either jockey shorts, which make them feel cozy, or boxers, which allow everything to swing around and get air.

Personally, I've taken the following steps to stop worrying about the aging process. I try not to bathe too often. Showers are preferable. Bathing poses the risk of seeing yourself in your entirety. I have often thought I resemble a landscape of cascading hills. In the tub, certain things are covering certain other things. I have to pick up stuff to get to other stuff. I once lost the soap in one of the hills, only to have it drop out during one of my lectures.

I don't buy pleated skirts anymore, as I've discovered that I am a pleated skirt. My bras are soft and comfortable. Let's face it: Is it worth getting traumatized over an illusion? At some point in time, the Wonderbra has to come off, and what ensues won't be so wonderful to view.

These things happen; we can't fight it. But whoever's up there in the sky has worked it out in His or Her wisdom. As you age, things double up. But then we can't see things as well either.

We need to honor our imperfections because they are part of who we are. They will allow us to resonate in the moment if we will only accept the fact that this is our own true nature. Tell yourself: *In every way, I think I'm such a treasure. And that's why I'm here—to give myself pleasure.*

Keep in mind that we are a youth-obsessed society. If we buy into this message, we forgo the wonderful part of aging, which is sageing. A sage shares his or her wisdom through being a mentor—a teacher and an inspiration to younger people. This can be through work, through Boy or Girl Scouts or other civic organizations, or informally with grandchildren or your friends' kids. You can teach younger people what you know or simply show them how to have a positive attitude. However you choose to mentor, I promise you'll get more out of it than they will.

This doesn't mean that aging is easy. You will need to sharpen your sense of humor, not lose what little you already have. Those who live to be 100 and beyond seem to be able to laugh at life easily and not take themselves seriously.

Extended life is not necessarily about trying to extend life in a solemn manner. I'm beginning to think my husband, Bob, really has a handle on the whole thing. He says, "What's the point of obsessing about your age? You probably won't remember how old you were when you died, anyway!"

So make a conscious effort to stop worrying about aging. After all, what's the alternative? Choose a few people who have a relaxed attitude about getting older, and interview them about how they feel and how they reached that mental place. People who age well and live long tend to have a positive attitude and a good sense of humor. Get together with a group of friends and have a good laugh at the aging process. Bypass the tomes on extending life, try to stop worrying, and work on developing a sense of humor and a positive attitude instead.

Relax, It's Only a Movie

Worrying is like reviewing a bad movie over and over. You know in your logical mind that worrying doesn't make anything better, but you can't help yourself. You interpret everything as if it's the end of the earth; and you create fear, tension, and stress wherever you go. If someone is ten minutes late for a meeting, you're sure he's had an accident. It couldn't just be the rush-hour traffic. If there's an airplane crash, you have to call all your relatives to make sure they weren't on the plane. In fact, I can relate very well to all this because I have my Ph.D. in Worry. I think I inherited the worry gene from my mother and my grandmother.

The Stress of Knowing

It's true that there are a lot of reasons to worry in our modern world. Most of the information we get from newspapers and television is awful—murder, drugs, political kickbacks, car crashes. A new trend is the publishing of memoirs that expose incest, physical abuse, and sexual infidelities. After a while, you start to think everything and everyone is horrible and that life can only get worse. But bad events have been happening since the beginning of time—remember the flood thing with Noah? Only back then, people didn't have the stress of knowing about it until long after it happened. Today we get the bad news from all around the world the minute it happens.

Even the weather contributes. Those five-day forecasts are real peace-of-mind killers. If today's nice, you get upset about the fact that it's going to snow on Friday. What if I die Thursday? All that snow will be the undertaker's problem. I will have gotten upset for nothing. Even if the weather is fine in your area for all five days, forecasters tell you about terrible national weather patterns. Now you can feel bad for people experiencing a tornado in Kansas and wonder if it's headed your way.

Of Mites and Men

Even if you have nothing to worry about, you can rest assured that some magazine or newspaper

98

article will inform you about things you had no idea existed, even in your wildest dreams. For instance, mites. These invisible creatures live on your body; you just can't see them. Hundreds of them are feasting on your skin and have condominiums on your eyelashes. There's probably a mall for mites under your armpits. Seen under a microscope, they resemble something out of the movie *Alien.*

Believe me, this is no joke. I get catalogs in the mail that have made a whole business out of this. Did you know that after six months your pillow has turned into a mite colony? That your bed has been converted to a landing strip for mites? And that many allergies can be attributed to mite bites? There are vacuums that suck them up and pillowcases and mattress covers that help ward off mite attacks. You could easily spend a thousand dollars on all the equipment you need.

99

After looking through the catalog, I started to wonder what to do when I travel. What about the mites that are left behind by people who don't believe in mite removal or who haven't been updated about this latest danger? Now not only do I have to worry about my mites, but there is a distinct possibility that when these mites commingle, they may not get along. Maybe that low humming I hear when I'm in hotels is really a whole bunch of mites fighting about whose bed it is.

This is only the tip of the iceberg. There is also bacteria on everything. Years ago nobody was interested in this stuff. If you got sick or cut yourself, you cleaned the wound, put iodine on it, and forgot about it. If it didn't get better, you went to the doctor, and he would make a simple statement: "It looks infected." Then he'd give you something to get rid of it—probably penicillin.

Now, because of all the articles on what we should worry about or watch out for, we have become pseudo-doctors. You could probably question a two-year-old now about her boo-boo, and she'd correct you and say it's a small puncture wound. Soon it will become impossible to leave the house without first encasing ourselves in a protective suit that has been completely sterilized.

As it is, you shouldn't eat meat because of mad cow disease and *E. coli,* which also can contaminate vegetables and fruits. You have to slather your entire body with sunscreen, wear a hat and sunglasses, but not before you spray on bug spray to prevent mosquitoes that may give you encephalitis from biting you. Now, I am happy that we are being given up-to-date information on the damaging effects of some of the above. But I find myself being too aware. I don't think there's a thing you can eat or drink that doesn't cause problems.

Even bathrooms are getting prime-time coverage. One newsmagazine show did 20 minutes on bathroom hygiene. They said to make sure that when you go into a public rest room, you don't use your hands to flush the toilet; use your feet instead. And don't touch the doorknob when you leave. So now I'm acting like a monkey, and I'm trapped in the bathroom because they didn't give instructions on the alternative for opening the door.

My mother really got into the whole bit about never sitting on the toilet seat. You were supposed to straddle the seat, not sit on it. This is an incredible challenge when you're in an airport rest room and you've dragged your luggage in with you. You're clutching your bag and trying to grab some toilet paper from these new Ferris wheel dispensers that should have a little voice inside that says, "Ha-ha, catch me if you can."

The next suggestion my mother gave me was that if you can't straddle, put tons of toilet paper on the seat in layers, then you can sit on it. But every time I've tried that, it all falls in as I sit down. Ah, now here's a new business idea: a spray for your rear end that will protect it from out-of-town bacteria. Then we won't have to straddle or wrap the seat.

Once again, we have to remember that fear and worry can become a way of life. There's only so much we can do; otherwise we have to become a walking can of Lysol.

Human Doings

At times it does seem as if our modern age makes it impossible not to worry constantly, not to be completely stressed out. Everywhere you go,

101

people discuss how much they have to do, and how little time they have to do it in. We've become human doings instead of human beings. Everyone's joined the Do More War, rushing around with lists of things that have to get done. People are like the White Rabbit in *Alice in Wonderland:* "I'm late, I'm late for a very important date. No time to say hello, good-bye."

Why is it so hard for us to stop doing? I believe part of it is tied into our overwhelming need to prove ourselves constantly. If we're doing something, we're validated. If we stop even for a few minutes, someone's bound to say, "Don't you have anything to do?"

102

If you find yourself running around like a chicken with its head cut off, worrying yourself to death, and never stopping to relax, you should consider taking up meditation. Take a few moments for a brief respite from the chaos of everyday living, and just sit and breathe.

Prayer can allow us to create an inner sanctuary as well. A woman I know says a prayer every night before she goes to sleep. She prays for every person she worries about—her parents, her children, her husband, and her friends. She prays for their health, for their safety, and for specific needs and concerns in their lives. She tells me that knowing she's said a prayer for each of the people she loves helps her not worry excessively during the day.

One of my favorite prayers is the "Clown Prayer" from *The Joyful Noiseletter,* the newsletter of the Fellowship of Merry Christians in Portage, Michigan:

> *Lord, as I stumble through this life, help me to create more laughter than tears, dispense more happiness than gloom, spread more cheer than despair.*
>
> *Never let me grow so big that I fail to see the wonder in the eyes of a child, or the twinkle in the eyes of the aged.*
>
> *Never let me forget that I am a clown, that my work is to cheer people up, make them happy, and make them laugh, make them forget momentarily all the unpleasant things in their lives.*
>
> *Never let me acquire financial success to the point where I will discontinue calling upon you in my hour of need, or acknowledging and thanking you in my hour of plenty. And in my final moment, may I hear you whisper: When you made my people smile, you made me smile.*

103

The Bottom Line

The shift from being to doing has been a slow but insidious process. Peace and quiet have been thrown out the window. Technology invades any place you can find to be alone. For instance, phones are placed in the bathrooms of many of the hotels I stay in. Corporate deals are now made on the john. This really is the bottom line! The phone is usually right next to the toilet. I eventually expect to see an ad that says, "Don't go alone, use the phone."

All this technology increases the pace and our sense of worry. You worry that you won't get your phone messages from your answering machine or that you won't return the calls in time. You worry that you didn't put fax paper into your machine and you might not get the important fax that's being sent to you.

So many of us have an overflow of work that we now have replicated our offices in our homes—we have computers, answering machines, and fax machines in our houses. We leave our offices, drive home, and then go right back to work, sometimes until midnight. Often we bring our paperwork home, just to remind us that we should be working. All weekend we know it's sitting there. It's like a little voice in our heads saying, "You haven't done your work!" This is probably a Committee member intruding into our thoughts. Our work is holding us hostage in our homes.

What memories do you want your spouse and kids to have of you? The moments your kids will remember are the spontaneous ones—the times you dropped whatever you were doing and said, "Let's go get some ice cream" or "Let's go toss the ball around." They'll remember this instead of your spending "quality time" with them—making the family yet another job that you have to do.

We need to spend more time doing simple, fun activities with our kids, and we need to buy them fewer toys. My grandmother Francesca used to give me a piece of bread dough to play with. She'd say, "Roll it!" She'd give me sesame seeds and tell me to put them on the bread, one by one. Do you know how long that takes?

Parenting with Humor

I've been asked over and over: How do you parent with humor? My standard response is: "I don't know how you parent with humor. I got my sense of humor back when my kids left." Naturally, that's not immediately helpful, but it does give us a reason to continue living.

Parenting is probably one of the most difficult things we'll ever have to do. Never mind the stressors associated with just trying to live your own life. Now we are taking on directing, managing, and being responsible for the outcome of someone else's life.

This is serious business, and it creates a lot of worry for parents. Simply stated, it means that we must somehow help to create an individual who can stand alone financially, socially, and emotionally. I'm always hearing about how difficult it is to raise a child in today's world because of drugs, media influences, and the pressures of being a two-income or single-parent family.

These are certainly valid concerns, but I believe they have been exacerbated by an excessive need to parent through a never-ending babble of pop psychology. It seems to me that so many of the parenting books have made the needs of the child paramount to the needs of the entire family. Creating respect for who you are may be one of the ways you can begin to reduce parental stress, and that in turn actually may loosen you up so you can enjoy your kids a little more.

A lot of the warnings we give to children are quite comical, although our intentions are to get across a serious message. Since I love irrational messages, I'd like you to think about some of the things you say to your kids that may be the very same statements your parents made to you. At some point you probably vowed you'd never let these words escape your lips:

106

- **"Why did you do that?"** What type of answer do we expect to get from this question? Do we think our kids will say, "I did it to drive you crazy, and I'm going to continue until you go completely insane"?

- **"Did you hear me?"** Parents usually say this in a voice loud enough to raise the dead. Of course your kids hear you—people in Outer Mongolia heard you. Your kids just aren't ready to listen yet.

- **"How many times do I have to tell you?"** Once again, what response are you looking for? "I think I'll do it 400 more times until you drop or can't count anymore"?

- **"You're going to hurt yourself! Don't come running to me when you break your leg!"** Now, think about that one. Doesn't this make perfect sense?

- **"If you run with that stick in your hand, you'll poke your eye out!"** Sorry, but you can't poke your eye out. You can poke it in, but you can't poke it out.

107

- **"I hope when you grow up you have children just like yourself!"** Well, I hope so too, unless they marry a cat.

- **"Laugh today, tomorrow you'll cry."** Wow, what a goal. I can't wait.

Role-modeling joyful, optimistic behavior is probably one of the best ways to get yourself out of the worry habit and to have a happier family with less stress. Sometimes we have no clue about how powerful our everyday conversations and body language are in setting the tone for our children's behavior.

When you drag yourself out of bed every day and tell everyone how tired you are, then you yell at your kids to get up, get dressed, and be cheerful while they're doing it, you're giving them a mixed message, at best. If you're hurrying around exclaiming what an awful day you're going to have, how much you have to do—and they'd better hurry, too—you've set the tone for tension and conflict before the day's even begun. If you and your spouse are yelling at each other, another layer of negativity and fear have been added to your kids' day. And if you put all your worrying onto your kids, they're going to see things in a pretty negative light. Parenting with humor and reflecting back to your children the joyful aspects of daily life means being willing and able to start with yourself.

Here are some ways to get rid of worry and add some humor into your family life. Make it your goal to move from common sense to nonsense:

1. Create a mission statement about what you value and what your purpose as a family is. Values might include honesty, courage, fidelity, kindness, respect, justice, and mercy. And don't forget to include having fun!

2. Provide a history of your family so that everyone can recognize his or her part in the ongoing process.

3. Model optimistic behavior as much as possible, and challenge your children's pessimistic views.

4. Celebrate for no reason at all. Have an unbirthday party, complete with cake and candles and balloons, for your kids. Have a picnic in the backyard for dinner. Put on music and dance to it with your children.

5. Act goofy with your kids once in a while. The older ones might get embarrassed, but it will show them that even though you're older, you can still act young.

6. Realize that your kids are home with you for only a short while, and you need to make the most of the time you have with them living under your roof. Take it from me: A few years ago, after 25 years of motherhood, my nest was empty. My youngest child, Erik (the culinary genius), went off to college.

Now I wake up to my own alarm clock, not my children's. Theirs used to beep continuously, waking me out of my slumber thinking a bus was about to back over me. What never ceased to amaze me was how consistently they were able to sleep through it and how I never could.

As a mother, there were many mornings when I wasn't able to get the kids up in time to catch the bus to school. Then of course I got to drive them. I did this many a time in my nightgown. My husband would just stare at me when I walked back into the house.

I have other fond memories, aside from freezing in my car in my nightie at 7 A.M. Many times I'd drive home after an evening meeting to find the house ablaze with lights and everything on, including the TV, the radio, and the food processor. The only problem was that no one was home! When I asked my kids why they felt we should be giving the electric company extra business, they responded by telling me they didn't want me to feel lonely when I came home. Their answers were always so logical.

Now when the phone rings, I know it's for me. There was a time when the only way my friends could get through to me was by homing pigeon. The phone cord is permanently stretched out to reach every room. It seemed that for my youngest son, no conversation was complete without constant pacing, combined with doodling. It was amusing to find the small profound messages written on anything he could get his hands on. I remember finding one written on the side of a Hubbard squash I was about to cook. Luckily, I saved the skin, since it had a girl's phone number on it.

Perhaps the hardest thing to cope with since my children moved out has been having a refrigerator that stays full longer. Not having to go to the supermarket twice a day to stock up has put me into a state of withdrawal.

To all parents reading this book who've given love, hope, and the gift of responsibility to a child, give yourself a pat on the back. You deserve it. Remember that the nest may be empty, but that bird is flying. And for parents who still have kids at home, appreciate those moments with your children. Don't waste your day with worrying. Before you know it, you'll be watching them walk down the aisle of their high school auditorium with those funny-looking mortarboards sliding off their heads.

111

Grown-Ups Are Missing Out on All the Fun

One of my favorite memories was my grand-daughter Amanda's second birthday party. Liz Taylor wasn't present, nor were any other Hollywood glitterati. There was no tent for the chauffeurs' cars, and the food wasn't flown in from Tasmania. It was just your down-home family get-together with good food and lots of child gawking.

My grandson Tyler, who at the time was 20 months old, was also present. This gave the adults the opportunity to focus on two kids for more than four hours. I don't know if you've ever noticed, but something happens to people when they're in the presence of toddlers. They become semicomatose and transfixed by everything the children do. The same thing seems to happen with dogs and cats.

Perhaps we are in awe of their playfulness and at the same time saddened by our loss of it. All adult eyes seem glued to the child's every movement, and each word uttered becomes a pearl of wisdom. We are sure, as we watch, that Einstein and Marie Curie are once again in our midst.

Adult conversation becomes sprinkled with "oohs" and "aahs." Profound statements are uttered, such as: "Did you see him pick up that bug? I can't believe it! Why, I wouldn't dare. Be nice to the bug." "She said she had to go potty. Isn't that clever?" "Did you fall down, big boy?" "Wasn't that fun?"

When it came time to eat, each child was encouraged to "Eat it all up, your mommy's waiting." Or "Here comes the train. All gone. Won't Big Bird be happy?"

As I watched the fun and games, I realized that being grown-up isn't everything it's cracked up to be. When's the last time someone watched you all day and oohed and aahed? And how many of us have tripped and been complimented? Normally the "big klutz" sign goes up, and it's usually followed by a smart comment, such as "Have a nice trip?" I've never been anyplace where a group of adults has tried to protect a bug. There has always been a united front to kill and remove the body as quickly as possible without any remorse.

I wonder if somehow we're not missing out on all the fun. It might be an interesting experiment to have a party and have everyone come as a toddler. We could make mud pies, play trucks and cars, eat and not worry about the food getting all over us, and even fall down and laugh about it. We could appoint someone the parent. Their role would be to hug and kiss us if we hurt ourselves, and tell us we're terrific every five minutes.

It could work, but then adults with their never-ending complexities would probably get analytical and turn it into group therapy, which would have to have results. I'm afraid it would become a job. But I, for one, am going to spend more of my time practicing what my grandchildren taught me—to laugh and live each moment to the fullest, as free from worries as possible.

113

Ta-Dah Number Six:
Turn on Your Imagination

Children have no problems being imaginative—just observe a group of kids playing pretend games. They aren't inhibited about role-playing and aren't embarrassed to act extravagantly silly in front of a crowd. A child's artwork is among the most beautiful creations on the earth. But somewhere along the way, we lose all our imaginativeness as our inhibitions and negative thinking take hold. By the time we're adults, we don't seem to have any imagination left—it's all been drummed out of us.

To recapture your imagination, envision your-self painting a picture or writing a book. What would the subject be? Where would you want your artwork hung? Who would you want to review or read your book? What kind of music would you write? Try keeping a journal, and write only fiction in it. Imagine taking a cruise all by yourself; what kind of stranger would you fall in love with? Imag-ine yourself having a fantasy romance with a pow-erful person in politics, or an actor or actress. Be very detailed in your fantasy—imagine what you'd say to him or her, and vice versa. Try to take at least five minutes a day to do nothing but imagine yourself somewhere else, doing something entirely different. This can make a traffic jam or a long line at the grocery store a lot easier to endure.

114

Our subconscious minds can't discern what's real and what isn't, so your imagination can help you fake it till you make it. Close your eyes and picture yourself jumping for joy, smiling, and feeling whole and content. Your brain will direct you to follow your imagination. Many health care professionals are using visualization techniques to help people reduce stress, anxiety, and fear. It's a directed form of imagination that can help us to maintain wellness.

෨෨ ෨෨ ෨෨   ෨෨ ෨෨ ෨෨

CHAPTER 7

LOSE YOUR BAGGAGE

So many of us are caught up not only in trying to find out who made us stressed and miserable but also in storing the information and cataloging it for future use. I call this "baggage handling" because after a while, we have so much past misery that we need suitcases to put it in. We may even need to hire someone to carry them if we have a whole set.

My grandmother Francesca was so good at recalling past history (mostly negative) that she could have been a curator for the Smithsonian. As a child, I would always ask her why she looked so unhappy. Her answer was always the same: "Because I suffer." She'd go no further, but her face would become even sadder and her hands would go up in the air as she recited one of her many invocations for God to help her in her hour of need.

There was always an aura of mystery around my grandmother's suffering, as if it were so unspeakable that it could only be alluded to in veiled words.

Every once in a while she would add a teaser: "My mother abandoned me!" This was all said in Italian, which adds such incredible drama. If she had said "My bra is killing me" in Italian, it would have sounded like a death knell.

I kept asking my mother to explain it to me, but she would slough it off with: "It's an old story, and you wouldn't understand." Years later one of my uncles gave me the whole scoop. It was indeed a good candidate for a made-for-TV movie. It seems Francesca's father died when she was 11, and after a year her mother married a man 20 years younger. This was virtually unheard of in Italy at that time. Because of the discrepancy in age and the fact that my grandmother was about to embark upon young womanhood, her aunts deemed that if my grand-mother lived with her mother and her younger husband, it would not only bring disgrace on the family, but there was also the possibility that he might become infatuated with her. And so Francesca was sent to live with her aunts, who lived next door.

Concetta, Francesca's mother, was always there for her, and her husband, Giuseppe, was a wonderful, gentle soul who did everything he could to make my grandmother happy. But even after my grandmother married and moved to the United States, bringing her mother and her mother's husband with her, she continued to treat her mother like the Black Plague. The abandonment issue became the centerpiece for her quilt of suffering. It never occurred to her that she could let it go and move on. Of course, this was made more difficult by some of the women in black that she hung out with. They reminded me of the witches in *Macbeth:* "Double, double, toil and trouble." Even though she did have cause for sadness, there was no need to color the rest of her life with a palette of gray.

So many of us spend our energies keeping lists on file of things people have done to us. It's as if we have a need to keep active those things that have made us feel bad. I do an exercise in my workshops that makes people realize their baggage-handling tendencies, and many are amazed at the outcome.

I ask them to choose a partner and describe all the negative things that have happened to them over the years. The partner listens and must respond with: "That's awful; tell me more." Then, when five minutes are up, the person has to describe all the good things that have happened. When I tell them to stop after five minutes of negatives, they all state that they could have gone on much longer. When I stop them after the positive sharing, most have been done for a while. They all admit that it was much more difficult to come up with the good stuff. Just think of your past week. I imagine that you probably have instant recall of the incidents that upset you, but if you were to think of the good things that happened, you would come up short.

It's important to differentiate between what you need to hang on to and what to let go of. Many of us have been severely traumatized by incidents from our pasts. History has taught us that if we don't remember the injustices, it is hard not to repeat them. Therefore, it is healthy to identify what has caused you pain, to gain insight, and, it is hoped, to move forward.

This isn't always an easy task, for those who have been emotionally wounded are also altered physically. For example, parts of the brain seem to function differently in those who suffer from post-traumatic stress disorder. We can no longer separate the mind from the body; one is witness to the other. There are many wonderful counselors whose entire practice focuses on healing events from the past. Don't wait to get help if you are suffering from a traumatic event. The pain won't go away by itself; that's one piece of luggage you should unpack with someone else.

Brain Drains

On the other hand, some baggage shouldn't even go into an overnight case. So many situations are just a brain drain. I often ask people to write down their stressors, and invariably someone will tell me how upset they get when a co-worker

118

takes extra time at lunch. One woman went on and on about how awful this was. I asked her how long this had been going on, and she responded, "Twenty years." So for 20 years she had been storing this nugget of information and informing her colleagues how angry she was about it.

I then questioned her about what type of action she had taken to try to resolve this. She responded that it was no use; no one would do anything about it. Now we have a great blend—a martyr with baggage. What never ceases to amaze me is how our behavior is so like a gerbil on its little wheel.

Of course, this gives others the power to manipulate your moods. You often use such phrases as "You make me . . ." (unhappy, angry, sad, upset). You say such things as "You drive me crazy; I can't stand what you did."

My own mother is a good one for holding a grudge. She could have auditioned for the part of Tony Soprano's mother.

When you have a lot of baggage, getting around becomes harder and harder. Anger slows us down in life. It's hard to think about work, have a conversation with the kids, or plan a vacation if all you're thinking about is the argument you had with your wife last night. This is one time you want to lose your baggage.

Once we are aware that someone's behavior affects us, we have some options. We can be direct and gently but firmly discuss the situation; we can change our attitude toward it; or we can let it go. Letting go is probably one of the most difficult actions a human being can do, since we love to squeeze the juice out of things.

Here are some ideas for baggage handlers to move from common sense to nonsense:

120

1. From time to time, try to reminisce about the things that turned out well. This type of thinking will create a greater sense of well-being and a more optimistic mood. I often recall my grandparents and what they did for me. The image of my grandfather pulling me along in my little red wagon to get ice-cream comes to mind often and makes me feel loved and very special.

2. Whenever you can't get past misdeeds out of your head, imagine what's troubling you as an ogre perched on your back. Yell out loud, "Get off my back!"

3. If there are pieces of your life that have left you saddened and unfulfilled, perhaps there is a way of re-creating those moments by finding surrogates who will make your life more fulfilling at this time. Many individuals would like to be adopted. Nursing homes abound with people who would love a visit from a

family member and who never get it. Perhaps there's a parent, grandparent, uncle, or aunt who can fit the bill, just waiting to be discovered.

4. Create a value system for yourself and your family. Having a value system helps you live your life in a more congruent fashion. Don't reprimand yourself with dialogue from your old baggage. Refrain from saying, "I can't get nuts in the car the way my father did," but say, rather, "I value inner peace and harmony so I will remain calm." Don't tell your children, "Clean up after yourself or you'll end up being a slob like my brother Joe." Instead, teach your children the value of responsibility.

5. Write your eulogy and epitaph. One of the most powerful things we can do is to think about how we want to be remembered. It gives us direction and purpose. Let's hope that when someone stands in front of those who will mourn your passing, he or she will be able to open that last remaining suitcase and find it filled with memories of love, laughter, and a life well lived.

121

List Keeping

For years my family was caught up in discussing who did what, when. Many of the good deeds people performed were lost in the quagmire of finger-pointing and self-righteousness. Don't we love to rattle off what others haven't done, while we religiously recount how we would never do that? Then we go into how much we have done for others, and what day and year we did it.

Perhaps because she is the oldest historian in the family, my mother has massive lists on everyone else. She can remember when I took my diaper off and what I did with its contents, how I kept her up at night, how many hours she worked to send me through college, and how I broke her favorite wooden spaghetti spoon. Mind you, she broke it when she smashed it on the table after getting mad at me for "behaving foolishly." (This was definitely a case of the pot calling the kettle black.) My mother could probably use a couple of trunks for her baggage at this point and a few Sherpas to carry them.

Over the years, I would get upset by her capacity for negative recall. I would counter by defending myself, desperately trying to deflect what I thought had brought on her displeasure with what I thought might bring her pleasure. This is usually a no-win situation. I always felt that no matter what I did, it was never enough. Eventually I came to realize that my mother's greatest wish is

122

for me to be a happy, successful human being. I know now that she was doing the best she could with the information she had on parenting.

This conclusion became easier to arrive at when I began to understand how I aided and abetted the process. When I stopped trying to salvage what I thought was my tarnished reputation (because, after all, I'm such a good person) and invested more time in seeing the humor in many of our conversations, things lightened up.

One example in particular always makes me laugh when I'm straightening my closets. Whenever my mother comes to visit, she does a military inspection. She tries to do it in an undercover fashion, because she knows that I know what she's up to. She might start by saying that everything looks nice. Then she may notice something new, and she'll tell me that I don't need it and that if I had gone through the Depression like she had, I wouldn't be so frivolous. Now, we're talking about a vacuum cleaner. "Why don't you just get an electric broom?" she asks. She has two—one from 1968 that just needs a little work, which I could have. Or I could sweep. That's what people did back then: They swept. The trouble with my generation is that we don't know the value of money. Wait until I get old and try to get into a nursing home. See if they'll take the vacuum in trade.

I thought I was in the clear at this point, but then she opened a closet and several hundred items fell out. When company's coming, I do exterior cleaning. I figure they're never going into the nooks and crannies. But not good old Mom. The head of Interpol would be outdone by her talents. Now we dug deep into the trunk for information on Loretta's past closet hygiene. She started with "This closet is a mess." Since I was familiar with the bait, I didn't bite. I just said, using one of my favorite assertiveness techniques called agreeing, "Yes, it is." "Well, you never did like to clean closets, did you?" she said. "No," I responded, "I never did."

Now she headed for the bottom of the trunk. "Remember when you were ten and I had to empty all your drawers and closets and we found things you thought you had lost?" She was getting a little closer to the marrow, but I held my ground. "Oh yes, I remember." How could I forget? In retrospect, the scene was right out of *Mommie Dearest.* Thank God I didn't have any wire hangers.

124

Her last remark was the impetus for what I thought was a most excellent comeback, even though it was tainted with sarcasm. She asked me what would happen if "they" came over and looked in the closets. Whenever you have this kind of pointless baggage, you probably have an entire cast to support your findings—something like Moses crossing the Red Sea. I looked at her in a somewhat bemused fashion and said, "It just so happens that I ran an ad in *The New York Times* about this closet. I said I was having limited showings. Ticket sales were so brisk that I decided to extend the viewings for another couple of weeks.

In fact, the Wednesday matinee has been oversold, and we may have to add another closet." The look on her face told me that I was about to get the lecture about being a smart-ass . . . but suddenly we both burst out laughing. It was an "aha" moment.

Ever since then, we have both been a little less focused on adding to the baggage inventory, although we do have relapses. The latest one occurred after my second PBS show. I asked my mother if she had seen it, and she said, "Yes." I said, "Did you like it?" She answered, "Yes, yes," but somehow it didn't sound convincing. I pushed harder and said, "What's wrong? You didn't like it, did you?" Finally after hemming and hawing, she spilled the awful truth. She told me I should never again wear the black blouse I had worn. And that if I didn't remember, she would remind me.

125

I literally almost fell off my chair. "Your daughter is on national television and you're going to store the black blouse in your memory bank?" Well, I thought, time for another "aha," or for some time in the witness protection program. There's usually no trace of you once you're in that. However, I quickly retorted that she had neglected to notice the scuff marks on my left shoe. This wasn't a good day for enlightenment, because she then reminded me that you only get one mother and that I'd be sorry when she was gone.

Dysfunctional Fame

The media aspects of baggage handling first appeared on talk shows in the 1980s, and became everyday fare for viewers interested in watching other people unload their trunks. It became fashionable for everyone, including celebrities, to confess. My grandmother used to call people like that *disgraziata,* the Italian term for "the disgraced ones." Back then you never ever aired your dirty laundry in public. Now not only do you air your dirty laundry, you sell it at a profit. Everyone is telling everything that ever happened to them. I wouldn't be surprised if one of the talk shows doesn't come up with a show on "How I became a serial killer after my mother stopped breast-feeding me."

Politicians, actors, actresses, athletes—anyone who has received public attention revels in sharing the intimate details of their lives. If they don't, someone is hiding in the bushes watching them so they can do it for them. Initially, we're appalled by the confession, but that reaction time is shrinking as "dysfunctional fame" becomes easier to come by than being known for something solid, such as sitting in a lab researching cancer. In about two weeks, the disgraced ones will have their own talk show or line of clothing. A combination of drugs, murder, alcohol, and adultery could land you on the cover of *Time* magazine.

Families used to do anything and everything to shield their good names. Yes, they unloaded their

126

baggage around one another, but they didn't invite strangers to do it for them. Francesca and her friends would have lit votive candles and said thousands of novenas for these poor souls' redemption.

In fact, my grandmother must be up in heaven, her halo of Italian sausages slightly askew, hands on her hips, wondering why Joey Buttafuoco or Divine Brown are getting movie contracts instead of a good beating. I can hear her now, asking me why so many people are publicly dumping their baggage instead of having a big plate of spaghetti and a few laughs.

Let's try to balance our negative baggage by storing up some of the joys and love we've gotten from people in our past. Maybe it's a former teacher who took extra time to help you through a difficult test, or a neighbor who always had your favorite cookie when you visited, or a parent who tucked you in at night and read you a story. There are always some good things that happen along the way.

127

Maybe we should pull the plug on television at night. Wouldn't it be refreshing to gather around and play a board game, or reminisce about some happy memories? Or how about a long, leisurely meal where everyone helps out and then tells about the good things that happened during the day? At the very least, try to pare down your luggage to a single overnight case.

Ta-Dah Number Seven: Tidy Up Your Life

Some of the biggest deterrents to peace and happiness are the daily messages we receive that tell us we need stuff to make us feel content. In the last 30 years, we've been trained to think that if we stockpile enough material goodies, we will reach some kind of high. However, once you get the dress, suit, car, house, or haircut of your dreams, you're seduced into thinking that something better lurks around the corner, and you'd better get it. We now have the It's-Never-Enough Syndrome. The wanting mind can never have enough, because it always wants something.

128

Take stock of what you have and take a sabbatical from buying to give yourself time to regroup. Take inventory of what you have and what you don't use. If you don't think you have a need for something anymore, give it to someone who does. How about clothing? Do you just buy to fill up an emotional hole? My mother always reminds me that during her younger days, people existed on very few outfits. Their spare money went into savings for their future. I often wish I had tempered my shopping in exchange for a bigger 401(k).

We often complain about cleaning and tidying up our homes. Perhaps if we pared down, we'd spend less time taking care of inanimate objects in exchange for caring for friends and family. Get rid of language that clutters your life, such as "I need that" or "I have to have it." You need respect, but you don't need a new lipstick or Game Boy.

Teach your children to give away toys they're not using, and restrict the amount of commercial television that tries to seduce them into pursuing the next fad of the moment. Thoreau knew what he was talking about when he said, "Simplify, Simplify." When all is said and done, you will leave this planet alone, and unless you're related to a pharaoh, you won't be taking your stuff with you.

❦❦❦ ❦❦❦

129

CHAPTER 8

GOING GLOBAL

Recently a woman in front of me in a grocery store line was beating a loaf of bread to death. She said, "Every time I come in here, it fills up with people!" I said, "Isn't that odd, the same thing happens to me." She said, "Something's going on." I said, "I notice the manager goes into his office and he calls people up. He's telling them to come here to see you and me." With that she got what I was aiming at, and laughed.

Do you recognize yourself in these phrases? "I'll never lose weight." "No one will ever love me." "Everyone gets waited on before I do." "I always get the slow line." If the weather is bad, it's because it's your day off. People came into the store because you decided to go shopping at that moment.

What you're doing is globalizing, and it's permanent and it's pervasive. The people who do this are into big-time suffering: "It never changes around here. I always get the slow line. Every time I go in there, it happens." First we presuffer: "I'm going to the store, and it's gonna be crowded." Then we get there and our dream has come true: The store is a nightmare. We've done our advance work, and now we actually get to suffer. Then we get home and review it so we can postsuffer. This takes away the opportunity to think about options. Perhaps we could enjoy the people at the store, or shop at a different time when it's less crowded. The most sensible thought is that if people didn't come to the store, the store would close!

132

Stop Global Whining

Postsuffering usually includes global whining. In order to get the most bang for your buck, you have to share the misery with others. Millions of people whine together all the time. If we expended the energy we spent on feeling bad about things, we'd have solutions to all of our problems.

People who globalize tend to use a lot of absolutes and overgeneralizations in their conversation. They think in terms of black and white. The gist of this is: The cards are stacked against me. The world is out to get me. I'm not allowed to be happy because the cosmic genies have it out for me. I was born unlucky, I'm unlucky now, and I'll always be that way.

People who think globally are good at what I call "multiplying by forever." That is, when things are bad, they believe they'll always be that way and that things will never change for the better. They feel hopeless, helpless, and depressed.

When you go on a job interview, do you tell yourself and your friends, "I know I'm not going to get it. I don't know why I bother"? When you get turned down for a bank loan, do you tell yourself that you knew you wouldn't get the loan, and you probably didn't deserve it? When your kids go off to college, do you tell yourself they'll call you only when they need money? If so, you're treading a dangerous path of negative thinking that can really get you into a ditch.

It's important to stop this kind of globalizing before it adversely affects your whole life. One way to combat this is to give yourself frequent reality checks. Is it really possible that your line at the grocery store is *always* the slow one? Look around; are people in other lines waiting a long time too? If you got into another line right now, would you hear the same complaints?

These little reality checks may sound self-evident, but if you keep at them, you'll begin to see that your overgeneralizations really don't work if you examine them logically. You need to check your glasses to make sure you're using the right lenses. The world is not out to get you; you are not the center of the universe.

133

Most of us don't realize what an impact we have on the world around us. Wherever you are, you can make a tremendous difference simply with your presence alone. Moods are contagious; you can affect other people's moods with your aura, your energy field. Have you ever come into your office and you're cookin'? You're smiling, you're happy, you're there. That positive energy field is going to affect others in your office in a beneficial way, even if you don't notice it at first. It's hard to be grouchy around someone who's up and smiling.

134

Why not ask for a standing ovation once in a while? When you go in to work, say, "I came in—it wasn't easy. I'd like a standing ovation." When you get home, walk in the door and say, "I'm back! I could have gone somewhere else, but I came home." And demand that ovation. The next time you go into the grocery store, ask everyone to applaud you.

Making life difficult is one way people avoid pleasures they feel they don't deserve. When we do stumble on happiness despite ourselves, we often begin to sabotage our happiness in order to get back into familiar territory. We can change these inner voices that haunt and repress us, but it takes conscious effort and a willingness to become more attuned to our thoughts. We also must realize that we are in control. There are many possibilities for change and growth—this is what makes life so exciting.

La-La Land

Remember when you were a kid and you got into your heavy staring? Your mother would say, "Come back! Where are you, in La-La Land?" By now you've probably buried or dismissed this wonderful place that can help us elicit inner peace and harmony. But as children, we daydreamed often and with great ease because we were so clearly focused on our intent and where we were at any given moment.

If children see a kite, balloon, or bird, they will zero in on it like sonar and track it with complete absorption. As parents, we often scurry after a small child who is following something that has become the object of his interest. It is as if he has become one with his object. This gets harder and harder to do as our minds become more and more cluttered with adult demands.

135

How often have you sat down for a few minutes to chill out, when you start hearing those nagging little inner voices asking, "Why are you resting? You know you don't have time for this! Get up, don't just sit there. You have lots to do. Keep going!" Children don't have those voices yet. That's why we have to keep telling them to clean their rooms, pick up their toys, and watch where they're going. They are so wrapped up in their delightful, adventurous activities, and so totally involved, that it's no wonder the universal mantra for parents is "Please look at me. I'm talking to you!" We hope that if they look at us, it will break the spell.

We all can learn to be spellbound again, to connect to that earlier experience called La-La Land. It isn't about writing one more report or finishing one more project but rather about becoming more in touch with the wonder of the universe.

I find that my garden draws me into this other world. When I'm there, I transcend time and space and let go of cares and concerns. There is nothing that puts things into perspective more than a squirrel that's trying for the hundredth time to get into a bird feeder with a cone-shaped top. Time after time it simply flips off and tumbles on the ground, yet without fail it tries again. It appears that the frustration is part of the game. For us, frustration is part of the struggle. I also realize there is a simpler, more majestic world, where phones don't ring and no deadlines occur. Not one bird in my yard has voice mail or an e-mail address. It appears that as we evolve, we also dissolve.

Take time to stare at clouds, stars, streams, flowers, people (politely, of course), kids playing, animals cavorting—anything that allows you to go to that wondrous place where time stands still.

The following are some guidelines to help globalizers move from common sense to nonsense:

136

1. Remain physically relaxed by stopping to do stretching or deep breathing throughout the day. Get plenty of exercise and fresh air. Occasionally take 10 or 15 minutes to get outside to take a walk.

2. Focus more on the moment-to-moment process of what you are doing and less on the end result, which will take care of itself if you are fully involved in the moment.

3. Let time be your friend and not a constant opponent. Do your best. That is all you can expect.

4. See yourself as a unique human being who expresses energy in a variety of areas.

5. See your work in terms of how it is helping others. By helping others, you're also helping yourself grow into a happier, healthier individual.

6. Laugh a lot with your fellow workers and with your family. Laughter creates a relaxing atmosphere and releases hormones that are good for you.

T.G.I.F.

How many of us are counting the minutes until 5:30 at the end of every working week? "Thank God It's Friday!" is echoed the world over by millions of individuals. It's a sigh of relief that the pressure is off and now we can play. And play we do! On Friday afternoons, bars are filled with people who begin relaxing by having a few drinks. Often the weekend is jammed with activities that we haven't been able to fit into an already over-crowded schedule. Some people play so hard that they're exhausted by the time they go back to work on Monday.

138

The attitude that work and play are separate entities and that they shouldn't commingle is one of the primary causes of stress on the job. We need to cultivate an attitude of relaxation and play toward our work if we are to survive our many years in the workforce. This doesn't mean that we must become passive, never trying to get ahead or improve our efficiency. It does, however, mean that we should begin to check out our underlying attitudes about combining work, play, and relaxation.

Expectations are common tension producers. We expect to get all our work done in a certain amount of time, with the complete cooperation of other people. This creates permanent tension because we are always waiting for the work to get done. Let's face it—all the work never gets done.

How many times have you heard a friend say that she's going to relax when all her work is finished? This type of individual usually is guilt-ridden when she finally does relax, and an inner voice constantly reminds her she didn't totally complete the work. When we focus all our energy on the final result, we never enjoy the process.

Who Are You?

Another area of tension comes from identifying ourselves too closely with what we do. Who are you? "I'm an executive." "I'm a housewife." "I'm a student." But we need to remember that we're not what we do. What we do is merely an expression of our energy. We have many different energies, and they can and should change throughout life. I continue to ask myself what I want to do when I grow up, and I hope you do, too. The key word is *growth*. Being open to change and growth gives us more options, thereby relieving a lot of tension.

139

Ta-Dah Number Eight:
Tap into the Universe of Humor

Here are some survival tactics that I like to tell people about, which help them find the humor in everyday life.

— Buy something silly and wear it. A Groucho Marx nose, mustache, and glasses are my favorite. Put them on in situations where you tend to see only the worst outcome. I wear mine when I drive through Boston, especially when I have to merge. People always let me in.

There are a lot of other places to wear silly things. Food shopping is one. Going to the dentist or the doctor, at staff meetings, or when talking to your mate or your children are other opportunities. When your mate's in a romantic mood and you're not, put on the glasses. Then say: "Start without me. When it sounds good, I'll be in."

140

When the stress seems unbearable, when you've really reached the limits of your endurance, go into a bathroom, look into the mirror, put on your glasses, and ask yourself: *How serious is this?*

— Have a "staff laff." Gather co-workers once a week and discuss some funny events concerning your own behavior. Putting other people down is not the purpose; creating a connection to our common absurdity is.

— Start a humor corner or a humor room at home and at work. If a DVD player is available, have some funny videos around. Make a basket full of silly hats, masks, noses, and wands. Put them on when you're having lunch, making dinner, or mowing the lawn.

— Do something nice when someone least expects it. For example, give that friendly receptionist a bouquet of flowers. Don't put a card in it. The big smile on the person's face will make it worthwhile.

— Write down your favorite profanities and then assign them a number. If someone is getting on your nerves, don't curse; just say the number. They'll never know. When your boss walks by, say, "Four." If your spouse or kids are giving you a hard time, say, "19."

141

— Be in the moment. Don't put off your happiness or your life for a better time. Remember, life is not a dress rehearsal, and it doesn't have to be a stress rehearsal.

— Adopt an attitude of playfulness. You don't have to do outrageous things, but keep your mind open to silly, irreverent, iconoclastic thoughts.

— Don't get caught up in "being funny." A sense of humor sees the fun in everyday things. It's more important to have fun than to be funny.

⊚⊚ ⊚⊚ ⊚⊚ ⊚⊚ ⊚⊚ ⊚⊚

CHAPTER 9

RELATIONSHIP KILLERS: THE BLAME GAME AND DIRECTORS OF THE UNIVERSE

There comes a point in a relationship where comfort sets in. Bob and I have been married 16 years. I remember the first time we were in bed together, lying there like two spoons. Bob got up to go to the bathroom and I called out, "Come back soon. Turn on the light so you don't trip!" Now, 16 years later, I'm on my side of the bed, waiting for him to come in so I can go to sleep. Bob has his ritual: flossing, gargling, and God knows what else for 15 minutes. Finally the light goes off. Then it goes back on. "What are you doing?" I ask.

"I gotta go to the bathroom!"

"Why do you need the light on?"

"What if I trip?"

"Who the hell cares!"

Things change, don't they?

The blame game can really make things sour in our sex lives. Now, I think we've gone a little too far in placing importance on sex in our society. It's gotten to the point that if you're in your 80s and you're not doing it twice a week, something's wrong with you. Demanding that you're going to have a romantic relationship is a false expectation that's only going to lead to unhappiness. Sure, you may have romantic moments, but if you can't appreciate the everyday life you have with your partner because you keep hoping for wine and roses, you need to examine your expectations to make sure they're realistic.

144

He Said, She Said—Who Cares?

There was a time when I didn't realize that men and women were different, except for the obvious. Now a day doesn't go by when I'm not reminded that we are definitely not working off the same page. The ultimate self-help book, *Men Are from Mars, Women Are from Venus,* has forever changed our perceptions of one another.

I used to think my husband was an idiot when he didn't answer me. Now I know he's just in his cave thinking—even though he's really in his chair reading the sports page, which is ultimately more interesting to him than my wondering out loud why he didn't take the garbage out. Years ago I would have gotten pissed off, taken it out myself, and then gone on to recite a year's worth of exact days and times when he hadn't taken it out. But now I'm supposed to be aware that men and women have different priorities. Maybe he's not in his garbage mode. Perhaps I can just get some seagulls to swoop in once a week, and that would solve the problem. However, those directions weren't in the book.

I also know now that men respond directly to what they are asked, since they are goal-oriented and want to get to the point. We women, on the other hand, like to explore, examine, and take a circuitous route to get to the same place. This was quite evident last week when Bob asked me how my friend Irene, who is in the middle of a divorce, is doing.

I began by answering, "Not bad," and then followed by asking him if he was sorry that we had gotten married. Then I asked him what if we hadn't—did he think he'd have been better off, and did he think if we'd waited it would have made a difference to our children, and would we have been thinner if we hadn't gotten married at all? He looked at me incredulously and said, "What the hell are you talking about?" Obviously he just didn't get it. I told him I knew he would respond this way because after all, he never cared for me anyway. I went on to comment that he probably never thinks about me at all.

Once again he stared blankly and said, "What is this all about?" I became more emphatic and asked, "What do you think about if you don't think about me?" "Well," he said, "I think about what fertilizer to buy for the rhododendrons, that I have to make an appointment to have the oil changed, and that I have to get ready to take a storewide inventory at work." "I knew it, you never do think about me!" I cried. All of a sudden he started walking out the door. "Where are you going?" I asked in my most patronizing voice. "To the hardware store," he said, "to get the fertilizer." "So that's it? You have no intention of admitting you were wrong?" "Whatever you say, honey," he replied. "I'll be back in a few minutes."

I immediately called my dear friend Myra, who knew exactly how I felt and who proceeded to validate me and assure me that this was simply male behavior. Other male traits have become more evident to me, such as my stepfather never wanting to stop for food, water, or the rest room when his course on a car trip was set. The objective was to get to the destination. I don't think Madonna standing stark naked on the side of the road would have made an impact on him. Getting there was all that mattered.

Men like to follow the plan. Women are more apt to stop here and there, chat and gather information, just in case they need to share it with someone else. That's why we spend so much time in the bathroom and why we all go in a group. Even if you were in Siberia and you didn't speak the language, you'd find a way to ask the woman next to you where she got her lipstick. Guys never go to the men's room in twos or threes. They have to appear in control and confident. Can you imagine a guy asking another guy in the next urinal where he got his suit?

I also have discovered that when my husband asks me how I feel, I can't take him literally. He wants a direct answer. If I say I've been having headaches lately, he'll tell me to make an appointment to see a doctor. Like a lot of women who have read their share of romance novels, I keep waiting for him to take me in his arms and fill me with romantic *bon mots,* saddened and filled with compassion for my unfulfilled dreams and unrequited love, promising to make it all up to me as we sail into the sunset. Lots of luck! In the very next sentence, he goes off on a tangent about some new bolt cutter he just bought.

147

I think it's time we all lightened up and realized that we can't control each other's behaviors or alter each other's personalities by dissecting every little thing with "genderspeak." Indeed, we should read, investigate, and educate ourselves to understand our differences. But you have to agree that if you did everything many of these books told you to do, you would have a 24-hour job. You'd end up too tired for a relationship.

One of the most desirable things you can work toward as a couple is the ability to laugh together, and often.

Here's what I call the ABCs of relationships:

- Accept other people for who and what they are.
- Be kind and considerate.
- Create a loving atmosphere.
- Don't criticize.
- Extract the best from each other.
- Forget about belittling your mate.
- Grow together.
- Hang out with positive people.
- Invite your loved ones into your heart.
- Join a cause together.
- Kiss, hug, or hold hands often.
- Laugh together until you cry.
- Move around, dance, walk, bike, and twirl.
- Nip anger in the bud.
- Open your heart to loving-kindness.
- Pick up a treat when it's least expected.
- Quit the need to be right.
- Record your blessings together.
- Stretch your capabilities.
- Treat yourselves to good health.
- Uncomplicate your lives.
- Vibrate with enthusiasm over suggestions and ideas.

148

- Wait to talk; listen first.

- Xerox loving quotes and share them.

- Yank hurtful words from your conversations.

- Zero in on being together as often as possible.

I'm Still Eating

Who's really in charge of your happiness? No one else can make you happy, nothing anyone else has done can make you unhappy, unless you misinterpret and decide you're a victim of other people. Then they have a great deal of power to make you terribly stressed and upset.

149

People who are into the blame game spend as much time as possible trying to find out who made them unhappy yesterday, today, or at some point in the future. If you've gained weight, you blame it on your family, your job, or the wedding you went to three months ago. Or on the fact that you have "big bones"—which makes you cousin to a dinosaur. If the Xerox machine is broken at work or the coffeepot is empty, you try to find out who did it and spend time reviewing this infraction with your colleagues. If you don't feel sexy, you blame it on your partner.

You're convinced that other people have a lot to do with how you feel: I eat because they make me nervous. I always have to eat when they make me nervous, and I've been eating for 40 years. They're dead now, but I'm still eating.

If they hadn't done what they did, you wouldn't feel as you do. That proves it: They're responsible for your feelings. You blame them and resent them. Sometimes you can get your own way if you can make them feel guilty for "causing" your hurt and anger. You assume that they knew their actions would hurt you, and therefore they intended to hurt you. This makes them terrible people and justifies your anger. You decide to teach them a lesson and straighten them out.

Of course, there are situations in life where we need to identify the culprits who have really harmed us. Try to identify them through therapy, and work on letting them go so you won't take them with you to your grave.

Here are some suggestions that move us from common sense to nonsense in our relationships:

1. Begin your day with loving-kindness, hugs, and acceptance. This is the best way to increase intimacy.

2. Celebrate your love often with words of encouragement, support, and delight.

3. Catch your significant other doing something right.

150

4. Motivate your mate to be who he or she is, not who you want him or her to be.

5. Laugh in bed as often as possible. This may not be "hot," but it will sure help you not to get too serious about your sexual relationship, and it will keep you from needing to assign blame when things are in a lull.

Who's in Charge?

151

Another area that's affecting our relationships is trying to be in control of everything. Now, there are a few things in life that we can control, but as time goes on, I'm finding less and less that I really can. One of the big wake-up calls that made me realize this was going through menopause.

I now have at least 50 books on the topic. I read that every three minutes, someone is turning 50 in this country. Ah, menopause . . . where there are no men, and certainly no pauses. The other day I asked my mother, who's 96, if she could give me an idea about when it might be over. She answered enthusiastically, "When you're dead." This, of course, was what I expected from someone who often responds: "You think this is bad? You haven't seen anything yet!"

I began to reflect upon when I first started my menopausal journey. I started experiencing symptoms in my early 50s, but then I found out that there is a perimenopause. This is when you have symptoms, but you don't yet know they are symptoms. Since I always feel a little weird and my friends and family consider me wacky, it appeared that I was merely becoming more of who I was.

The first clue I had that something was going on was when my abdomen began to resemble a small zeppelin, and I tried to make coffee with the toaster. Each week something new would emerge. Phone numbers and people's names would escape me, pounding headaches would come and go, my heart would race like an engine, then go back to normal, only to skip a beat. My skin became reptilian, my hair stood on end, and my tolerance for anything was at ground zero.

I began to plot how to get a contract out on my husband, whose breathing had become an incredible source of irritation. Keep in mind that this is a man who literally has the patience of a saint, a great sense of humor, and makes very few demands. I decided none of this mattered; it was the breathing and the way he chewed lettuce that were at the root of my problems.

I began to share my experiences with other women and heard similar stories of lowered libidos, dry parts, no waistline, sagging breasts (this is not a pretty sight; mine were already at half mast), brittle nails, and the ever-present hot flashes. The hot-flash stories were ominous, to say the least. They ranged from small, quick feelings of being overheated to wringing out the sheets in the middle of the night. I had somehow escaped the flashes, but my Committee reported that there would be hell to pay with some other symptom. The only thing I didn't hear about were fallen arches. But then who knows, I'm sure somewhere in some subterranean lab, someone is studiously trying to correlate fallen arches to a lowered estrogen level. I pity the poor mice who are walking on a treadmill in high heels while someone takes their hormone levels.

I finally hit the wall when I started waking up at night at 2 A.M. This was not your ordinary awake, but a hyperawake state that would be appropriate for guarding a nuclear warhead. I would try to go back to sleep, using my wealth of relaxation methods. But of course I'm also fighting a mind that is continually questioning what's going on. So while I'm trying to relax, I'm asking myself, *I wonder when I'll get back to sleep,* or telling myself how tired I'm going to be if I don't. The longer I stayed awake, the more terrorist information I fed myself until I was not only wide awake but also a nervous wreck.

Since I'm obsessed with knowing things, I bought the first of many books on insomnia. One of them said it was a good idea not to lie awake in bed, but rather to get up and read a boring book until you got sleepy. The most boring book I could find was my car manual. I didn't get sleepy, but I finally learned how to work the fog lights.

153

Another book said to make snacks. They had to be carbohydrates so they could trick your brain into believing it was tired. English muffins, pancakes, waffles, popcorn: These were now part of my nightly ritual. An English muffin and the car manual—what a treat. Meanwhile, every day I had to teach groups of people how to use humor to reframe stress. The bags under my eyes looked like they hadn't been unpacked for weeks. I had gained weight from the thousand or so muffins I had eaten, and I had put a deposit down on a hit man. I sought help after I ended up in Pittsburgh to do a lecture that I was supposed to give in Philadelphia.

154

After I got back, the first thing I did was to go to see Barbara, a friend of mine who's a therapist. She gave me some wonderful advice. She asked me why I needed to make staying awake into such a pathology. She said, "Try to enjoy the time you're awake. You may discover some interesting things about yourself."

Being the control freak that I am, I was doing what so many of us do. I was commanding myself to fall asleep. The mind is an insidious little saboteur. The more we demand that it do something, the less it cooperates. Only when we let go and allow ourselves to be with what is happening does true change occur.

Barbara also suggested the obvious: Go see a doctor to find out if hormones would work for you. Why hadn't I gone before? Because, once again, it was an issue of control. I don't like to take medicine because once that pill goes down, I don't have any control over it. I finally decided to see a physician. After a thorough examination, she reported that yes indeed, I should take hormones. I left with a trusty prescription in hand, ready to confront and reverse the damage done by my estrogen depletion.

I dutifully had it filled and went home to read the printout the pharmacist gave me on possible side effects. Once again this was going to create a problem for me. When I hear the word *side effects,* my anxiety level automatically rises. My control freak mentality rears its ugly head and I start thinking about how I'm going to control the side effects or, worse still, how I might die a slow, agonizing death from them.

155

As I read the printout, I became more and more convinced that I couldn't cope with what might happen as a result of taking the hormones. Now I needed to use a little common sense here, and realize that the percentage of people who suffer from side effects is small. But you see, I know, since I am the Grand Poo-Bah of the entire universe, that I and I alone will have the greatest number of problems.

One side effect finally made me laugh out loud. Part of the perks of taking HRT (that's what you call it if you're in the know) is that it makes your dry parts juicy. The last side effect listed, which probably occurs in one in a million cases, was the possibility of a blood clot that could create a stroke, which in turn can leave you with brain damage.

Well, I thought, here's the cure and the curse. Your parts are juicy, but now you don't know it.

I have tried an herb called Dong Quai, acupuncture, massage, chanting, mud baths, and soy products. Soy is thought to help reduce some of the symptoms because it contains phytoesterols, which are natural estrogens from plants. The bad news is that eating soy is similar to taking a nap on a sheet of sandpaper.

Last week I was finally rescued from my menopausal fixation by two things. First, I saw a T-shirt that said, "I'm Out of Estrogen and I Have a Gun." Second, I read about a new study that assured women who had decided not to take estrogen that it was never too late. The article said that taking it after 60 may actually be more effective and that the reward may be fewer side effects. What a relief—one less thing to be in charge of.

By the way, they've discovered that men go through menopause, too. Now that I think about it, that's probably why I can't find the car manual!

I've had many opportunities to question why it is that so many of us have tendencies to be Control Czars or Directors of the Universe. I don't have the entire answer, but think for a moment about how we're brought up. For the most part, it's been by direct command. We were told for the most part to "Do what I say, not what I do." So naturally once we're grown, we want to be the ones directing things.

Just Leave the House!

My mother, who has an incredible sense of the ridiculous, was remarking on our desire to control things. She commented on the fact that nobody seems to be able to do anything anymore without someone telling them how to do it. She mentioned that since everyone is getting so entrenched in what experts think, pretty soon they won't be able to leave the house without asking someone's advice. She figured she'd make millions by just writing one word: "Leave!" Of course, she also managed to point out that people hired me to learn how to laugh at their stress—something that her generation did automatically, along with consuming their spaghetti and wine.

It appears that there is absolutely nothing a human being does that doesn't have a self-help book attached to it. If you're talking to someone, it's no longer just a conversation. If it's a man, we can't talk to him the same way we talk to a woman because he hears things differently. If you don't say it the right way, he might wash the car instead of changing the baby's diaper. If you're having a fight, you have to stay away from words that could trigger old wounds.

My grandparents didn't give a hoot about old wounds. They just yelled back and forth at each other. "*Fatti, I fatti tuoi!*" my grandfather would shout ("Mind your own business!"). "*Sei pazzo!*" Francesca would respond ("You're crazy!"). Finally

157

one of them would say, *"Ho fame!"* ("I'm hungry!"). The whole thing would end as abruptly as it started, and they'd become absorbed in getting the water to boil for their daily plate of spaghetti. They were married for over 50 years without ever attending a couples' workshop.

Nowadays, however, we want to control every single aspect of our lives. We can take a seminar on everything, from how to manage our anger to how to walk right. It amazes me that there are entire tomes on walking properly. What has happened to all the people who are walking incorrectly? Are thousands of them showing up in emergency rooms traumatized by injuries because they were walking wrong?

158

There are also books on breathing, baby-sitting, recovery, and hundreds of books on weight loss. It's not that I don't see the value in the information we have accrued to help humanity overcome itself. But we do need to get a grip on what we can control and what we can't. Some things are okay just the way they are. Can you imagine an entire race of individuals who had absolutely nothing wrong with them? Forget it; it wouldn't last five minutes. Somebody would write a book, *Returning to Dysfunction: The New Paradigm for the Modern Thinker.*

Jackie Mason, one of my favorite comedians, has a great story about therapy. He said he went to a psychiatrist because he was having trouble trying to figure out who he was. The shrink said, "We can do it, but it's going to take some time and may cost you a lot of money." Jackie responded, "Hey, maybe I'm you, and you owe me money."

I'm My Own Fault

My sense of the absurd is never more present than when I'm leafing through one of my many New Age magazines. I just can't wait to see what someone's going to come up with that needs either channeling, changing, or recharging. It's ironic that so many people who turn to New Age workshops and spokespersons to soothe and heal their lives often become obsessed and stuck in the process. I've also noticed that they become very serious about the particular method—how it must be done, and who they must do it with. Once again we believe that by doing things in certain ways— particularly if they are shrouded in mysterious language and are attached to rituals—we will gain control over our entire beings and, if we're lucky, avoid death.

Unfortunately, this type of thinking has a very harmful side effect. You begin to feel bad that you didn't do whatever you were told to do, in the manner in which it was told. Now not only are you screwed up, but you feel bad about it. This kind of guilt doesn't seem to be as prevalent in Western medicine, because for the most part, health care providers use language that is fairly straightforward.

159

On the other hand, some New Age authors and seminar leaders speak as if they've been informed by a higher source. The higher source often has a name you can't even pronounce, such as Matu or Xanthua. The source has found someone to talk through, to give wisdom to the rest of us dribbling idiots.

I often have wondered how Matu chooses whom he wants to use as his human container, and why he's never come to my house. How does the selection process work? Does he have a Rolodex on his desk, or does he have a meeting with the other sources and they all decide together? Is there a union for these higher beings? Who's on the board of directors?

As a result of all this New Age mystery and navel-gazing, pondering becomes a way of life. Now, I'm a firm believer in investigating, philosophizing, and having a heightened sense of curiosity. But too much pondering can diminish your sense of delight and joy. I know people who won't go to the bathroom until they clear it of bad energy. They have to wear "pure" clothing that's woven by Hindus from ancient nomadic tribes, adorn themselves with charms that have been blessed by holy water from the Ganges, and go into a long chant if you say something negative.

One of my acquaintances has gone through so many transformations that she now fancies herself to be some kind of guru. No matter what you say, she has something in her bag of tricks that will heal you. I happened to mention that I had a wart, and I got a 30-minute lecture on why I got it. It seems that in my past life, I was married to my mother, who was then the King of England. In this past life I didn't feel empowered, because women weren't considered valuable. As a result, I had unresolved issues. I now had the wart as a symbol of not being able to express myself. She knew this was true because the wart was on my middle finger, and the body never lies. I decided not to get rid of it because, who knows, I might need it in my next life for something else.

At times a sense of arrogance is attached to all this knowing that puts us at a distance from those who are not in the know. It's similar to humor that excludes people and leaves them out of the circle that's in on the joke. We already have enough problems with separateness, what with racism, ethnic differences, and questions of sexual preference. Let's not add being so evolved we've left the planet.

161

Here's a list of fun self-help book titles that no one has written. Keep in mind that irreverence is a wonderful part of humor:

- *Quantum Carpooling: Always Gets You in the Right Lane*

- *I'm My Own Fault: Recovery for One*

- *Enough Already: For Those Trapped in the Cycle of Getting*

- *Ageless Body, Empty Mind*
- *Voice Mail: Where Gender Doesn't Count*
- *Oy Vey: The Universal Whine*
- *Wherever You Are, You're Not Done*
- *Chakras I Have Known and Felt*
- *Collective Bullshit: The Journey to Self-Importance*

When the emphasis on self-improvement becomes a full-time job, we must realize that we're trying too hard to control our lives and those of others. In our attempts to wake up, we may have fallen asleep.

162

Director of the Universe

Another aspect of trying to be in control is telling others how to do things. In my own quest to be Director of the Universe, I convinced everyone that I could organize anything from a dresser drawer to a presidential campaign. My house could have passed a military inspection. Socks with socks, knives with knives. Spoons could not commingle with forks. This would have been the end of the world as we know it.

My home was only the tip of the iceberg, because when you're a Control Czar, you also like to direct other people's lives, even though they may not be interested in your doing this. It's like being the head of a home improvement committee. You know that others could profit greatly from your profound words of wisdom and wealth of knowledge, which you are willing to share with these poor unfortunates who are somehow missing that part of their brains.

Becoming a single parent and working full-time not only changed the course of my life, but it also left me with a lot less energy for the rules I had imposed on myself. My new status altered my need for order and my need to observe and judge other people's disorder. When I remarried, I remained less organized, but I still made sure that my husband's socks were in his sock drawer and his clothing neatly lined up in his closet.

163

As my career flourished, my thoughts became less and less involved with drawers and closets. However, this was distressing to my husband, who was used to a woman who did it all. When I asked him to help, he responded that he didn't know how to do the laundry, cook, iron, or go food shopping. I tried to be understanding; after all, he came out of the 1950s, when real men didn't do such things. And he handled other chores, such as washing the cars, fixing leaks, hanging pictures, and mowing the lawn, all the while working full time.

The grass cutting was a job in itself. I would have traded folding underwear for mowing, but he'd have none of that. I didn't have the right lawn training. He would tell me how neat his rows were and that when he'd allowed me to mow, I had left tufts—a sure sign of erratic mowing. I countered by saying that no dog in the neighborhood had reported the tufts in its trips across our yard. He found this less than amusing. Week after week we jousted over who was going to be in charge of what. If he attempted to do one of the things I thought he should do in our modern two-income family, I would inspect and try to educate him about how I would have done it. He would respond in kind. And so our duet became "Try it, and I'll test you."

After one particularly stressful week, I woke up one morning to a lot of banging and sighing. "What's wrong with you?" I inquired.

"I don't have any socks or underwear. What am I going to do?" he responded. I was just about to give all my old tired responses: I just couldn't get to it, I planned to do a wash that evening. Instead, I answered, "Why don't you wear mine?"

That remark clinched it for my husband. Before long, from somewhere deep in his seat of knowledge, he discovered skills he thought never existed. I would hear the washing machine running, only to think *How could that be? I'm the only one who knows how to work it!* Yet there he was, deftly measuring soap into the small measuring cup just for laundry detergent. He suddenly seemed to know exactly how much and what kind of soap to use. His food shopping skills escalated into something Martha Stewart would be proud of, and stacking the dishwasher became an art form.

A strange thing started to happen. The more savvy he became about househusbanding, the more time he took to lecture me when I did the very same chores. He was becoming a Director Extraordinaire. When I loaded the dishwasher, he would assume his folded-arm stance and proceed to tell me that the plates were not tilted in the right direction. I got weekly reports about the lint filter in the dryer, and he began to clip coupons from the newspaper. I knew something had to be done when he told me I needed to stop leaving dishes in the sink. Finally, after a night of exchanging remarks on who did what and when, we decided that neither one of us had to be in charge; we just needed to work together to make life easier for the two of us.

165

Of course, we are not unique. I've heard thousands of stories from people who are unwittingly doing the same things. We try to control conversations, the way people drive, how they think and feel, and, if possible, how they feel about us. One of the biggest lessons I've had to learn is that I cannot control everything and that I'm not in control of anyone.

My children were my best teachers. Often we think that we can direct them and advise them, and they will follow our lead. Some do, but then there are those who decide very early on to have minds of their own. My daughter, Laurie, is the latter type. The two of us could have been in charge of the world, only we would have an ongoing debate about who the chairman was. In between vying for the position of Most Knowledgeable, we become convulsed about how funny we are. Even though we've had our mother-daughter conflicts, I've had some of my best laughs with her. The kind that leave you immobile, doubled over, and convinced you are going to wet your pants. Once again, the saving grace becomes the ability to let go and realize that control is a matter of perception, and that it can change in the blink of an eye or in the middle of shared laughter.

Ta-Dah Number Nine: Try to Be Different

166

Unconventional people do not take themselves too seriously, and that usually puts them in the mood for a good laugh. The next time you feel like doing something wacky, go ahead. "Eccentrics are healthier," says David Weeks, Ph.D., a neuropsychologist at the Royal Edinburgh Hospital in Scotland who has spent ten years studying oddballs. Among other findings, the people Weeks studied went to doctors only $\frac{1}{16}$ as often as other adults.

Inside every person lurks a little bit of wackiness. Let your quirky side out once in a while. If you work at a conservative bank or law firm, wear a tie or scarf with just a bit more flair than is the norm. Your underwear always can be unique because nobody sees it (at least at work). Get yourself a business card for friends and family that gives you an unusual title: Goddess of Guffaws, Director of

Everything, Inverse Paranoid. Have a menopause party or an unbirthday party. During the flu season, have a flu party. Walk out of your bedroom backward. Stand on one leg when you're talking to a higher-up. The important thing is to step outside of the box you've put yourself in or to remove the safety net you've covered yourself with. The brain appreciates the stretch. Your mind needs new and different ways to think. Don't get into a rut. The reward for your limitations is that you get to keep them.

◎◎ ◎◎ ◎◎ ◎◎ ◎◎ ◎◎

CHAPTER 10

HOW TO PREVENT HARDENING OF THE ATTITUDE

Many times after I've finished speaking at a workplace, a handful of people come up to talk to me. A few will hang back until the others leave, fearful, I'm sure, that they will be overheard. Do they have some dreadful information about a possible takeover that no one knows about but them? No, they just want to confide in me that they finally feel validated; that they feel optimistic most of the time and they have fun and laugh whenever they can. Then they add that they also get their work done.

It's sad that these individuals often are perceived to be unrealistic and that they "just don't get it." Daily, many of them are asked questions, such as "What are you so happy about? Haven't you heard about what's going to happen around here soon?" When they respond with "I heard, but I'm going to focus on making the best of it," they are looked at as if they're crazy.

It's amazing how many of us focus on what's wrong instead of what's right. Millions of dollars are spent annually to send employees to workshops entitled "How to Deal with Difficult People." Wouldn't it make more sense to send the difficult people to workshops on how to be more reasonable and optimistic? Whoops, I almost forgot, that borders on a more rational way of thinking. I suppose it's just as ridiculous as suggesting that every workplace have stress-management programs. As one corporate executive told me, "It's not cost effective." I asked why, and he replied, "Because you can't prove absence of death." Okay, "Whatever," as my eight-year-old grandson Nicholas might say. I've found that this phrase is a great way to deal with things that make no sense, or when you just don't have the strength to refute something you know is idiotic.

170

I was handed the following one day by an employee whose company was "downsizing" (a word I think works better for dieting):

We the willing
Led by the unknowing
Are doing the impossible
For the ungrateful.
We have done so much
With so little
For so long

We are now qualified
To do anything
With nothing.
— Anonymous

Optimists Live Longer

According to research by psychologists at the University of Minnesota and the University of Illinois, no matter what happens, people tend to return to a genetically fixed level of happiness. David Tellegen and David Lykken at Minnesota found that twins shared a "characteristic mood level," even when raised separately.

Yet those who believe that heredity may be a basis for happiness also say that it doesn't mean a person can't change. Much of the pessimistic behavior we witness in ourselves and others is really an unwillingness to embrace change or, at the very least, to have a better attitude toward it. Our attitudes stem from our beliefs. If we believe that it always rains on our day off, that the particular plane we're on is probably going to crash, that the grapes we just ate will probably kill us, then we have a good chance of feeling helpless and miserable. We're likely to think *What's the use, we have control over nothing.*

Now, I am not advocating being a Pollyanna. Pollyannas are passive and ineffective: Everything is just dandy; no problems anywhere. As the lava

171

from Mount Etna is licking at their shoes, they say, "Isn't this great? A hot time in the old town tonight!" The moderate and more healthy stance is to recognize that, yes, it may rain on your day off, but it's still a day off and you can enjoy yourself. Yes, planes crash, but you can choose not to fly or take a course in how to deal with the fear of flying. And the grapes and a hundred other things could kill you, but that's the way it is. You can accept it or move in with Michael Jackson.

172

Keep in mind that people are rarely 100 percent optimistic or pessimistic. Most of us are somewhere in the middle of the continuum. Our optimistic nature may also be sorely tested; even though it has been our practice to look on the bright side, assaults to our self-esteem may provoke us to become more pessimistic. Yet more often than not, we return to our usual way of being. I am happy to report that pessimists can become more optimistic. And it can be done by not turning the proverbial molehill into a mountain. There may even be a chance that optimists live longer. Pessimists are accurate, but they don't live as long!

Here are some ways to become more optimistic:

1. Anticipate that something unexpected could happen. Most things don't always work out 100 percent. If they do, be grateful; if they don't, consider it an opportunity to challenge your ability to problem solve. Try to consider as many

options as possible. If the human mind has the capability to land a vehicle on Mars, it should certainly know what to do about a hangnail.

2. Accept some things as they are. For instance, I'm short and I'm never going to get taller. The more I agonize about my height, the shorter I feel. It's more than likely that I'll get even shorter as I get older. So why should I feel awful about something like this? How can I prevent hardening of the attitude over the things I can't accept? I could get on a rack and torture myself into stretching another half an inch, but then what? My height is what it is! And much of life is like that.

173

3. Live your life with meaning. Give your life direction and a sense of purpose that makes you want to greet each day with enthusiasm and excitement. There is no direct path to discovering a sense of meaningfulness. Some people are fortunate enough to discover it very early in life; some, later on. It can be found through work, through experiencing someone or something, or through circumstances that appear to have absolutely no meaning because they are inherently tragic. This of course is the

most difficult way, but there are those who have traveled this path and have turned tragedy into triumph to become some of our greatest role models. (Consider, for instance, Maya Angelou, Christopher Reeve, Elie Wiesel, and Viktor Frankl.)

4. Live mindfully. Be available to the here-and-now. Try to look at each situation with new eyes. This is often difficult when we have pessimistic beliefs. Many of our ideas are supported by a larger belief system that can date back to our childhoods. Even though it may no longer work for us, we still may prefer our old belief system because it feels comfortable. This is why it's so important to review our Committees and the messages we have gleaned from them.

   Telling people to look on the bright side will often just get you a history lesson on why they feel the way they do. Try to keep the focus on what's happening now and, more important, to be present to it. The following narrative by an anonymous author probably expresses it best:

174

Chapter One
I walk down the street. There is a deep
    hole in the sidewalk.
I fall in. I am lost . . . I am helpless.
It isn't my fault.
It takes forever to find a way out.

Chapter Two
I walk down the same street. There is a
    deep hole in the sidewalk.
I pretend I don't see it.
I fall in again. I can't believe I'm in this
    same place. But it isn't my fault.
It still takes a long time to get out.

175

Chapter Three
I walk down the same street. There is a
    deep hole in the sidewalk.
I see it is there.
I fall in . . . it's a habit . . . but my eyes
    are open. I know where I am.
It is my fault. I get out immediately.

Chapter Four
I walk down the same street. There is a
    deep hole in the sidewalk.
I walk around it.

Chapter Five
I walk down a different street.

5. Set realistic goals. If you're always putting yourself down about your weight, your job performance, or your relationships, choose one and start writing down some positives. Pessimists work best with evidence. If you can't find anything positive, ask someone who cares for you to help.

Reframing

Throughout this book, I hope I've helped you see that you can shift your perspective on situations that distress you and begin to see opportunities to become more optimistic, joyful, and resilient. When we shift our perspectives, we have reframed a situation and have allowed ourselves to see our world through a clearer lens. Many of us reframe in a negative way, which essentially gets us what we don't want. We would rather spend years of our precious existence being more upset than look at or change the one thing that is so obviously available to us, which is our thoughts.

Humor is one of the most natural ways to reframe. It forces the mind to loosen its grip and opens it to new understanding. In other words, we "get it" before it "gets us." Naturally, I realize that we can't do this in every stressful situation. However, in the everyday living of our lives, we must all admit that we could take ourselves less seriously.

Making Things Better by Making Them Worse

One of my favorite ways to do this is through the art of exaggeration, which is a natural way to reduce stress and anxiety. The reason this works for most of us is that we've been doing it most of our lives—except that we took our thoughts to new levels of fright instead of delight. A study by Michelle Newman, Ph.D., shows that almost anyone can reduce negative responses to stress by mentally writing an impromptu sitcom of sorts—even those who consider themselves to be humor challenged. One of the reasons we laugh at Bill Cosby, Billy Crystal, and a host of other comedians is that they allow us to see our absurdities in such a way that we become more compassionate toward ourselves and others.

177

Reframing our negative thoughts through humorous exaggeration sends a vital message to the brain that says: "Hold it, I really don't need to get ready to do battle today. Instead, I'm going to take a shower in endorphins and assume this challenge with a calm, somewhat bemused mind."

Let's look at some typical situations that I hear about all the time and see how we might reframe them through exaggeration:

Family Chores: No one ever helps me around here. I have to do everything myself. I'm sick to death of being the only one who cleans up.

Reframe: This house is the worst snake pit I have ever seen. You're all out to get it condemned by the Board of Health. Dirt balls are taking over the bedrooms and giving birth to more. It's not a problem though, because I'm putting the whole house on the curb for the garbage men.

At the office: I knew it; they're giving me extra work since they laid off Janet. What do they care? I'm nothing to them. I'm overworked as it is. What am I going to do now?

178

Reframe: I don't know why I'm surprised by them giving me more work, since I know everything anyway. By the time I'm done, they'll find me buried in memos. I'll end up in the dead file, and they'll hire someone new to do Janet's and my jobs.

In traffic: This lousy commute is going to kill me. It's the same damn thing every day. Look at that moron weaving in and out. Boy, am I tense.

Reframe: It's a good thing that I'm the only one who knows how to drive the right way. If traffic stalls, I might have the chance to get out of my car and give some of these incompetent people some lessons. Maybe I'll even get a new job as Director of the Highway. God, I'm good!

Take a few minutes to think of some situations that you could reframe.

Just Stop It!

I can make myself really go off the deep end by playing and replaying conversations in my head or by going over something that might happen. My inner saboteurs love to tease and torment me. I particularly hate injustices, and I will spend precious moments playing the Ping-Pong match of who said what, the fact that they shouldn't have said it, and how unfair it is. I can get into this almost to the point of obsession, like a song you hear that you just can't get out of your head no matter what you do.

I find that talking to myself helps a great deal. We often forget that we're our own best friends. Taking the responsibility to intervene on your own behalf is a very important part of breaking the cycle of distress and anxiety. When you find yourself awfulizing and catastrophizing and you want an immediate reaction, just yell, "Stop it!" or "Shut up!"

Now, the irony is that you're yelling at yourself for having thoughts you can't control. However, doing this appears to have some magical properties and seems to startle the mind into obeying. You need to be forceful and loud and, if possible, to use expletives. Obviously, this precludes using the technique when you're at a social event or in church. But it's great when you're at home (barring the presence of children), and it's wonderful when you're in your car or out walking or jogging.

179

Recently I was taking my daily walk, and I had gotten into one of my internal conversations that was going nowhere. I decided to take some forceful action. I hadn't noticed that one of my neighbors was standing close to the road, watering one of his bushes. I yelled at the top of my lungs, "Stop it, I'm sick of you!" He turned a deep shade of red and dropped the hose. He looked in my direction and began mumbling apologies about just finding out about the watering ban and that he hoped I wouldn't tell anyone. I muttered "Okay" and quickly walked away, because I was about to burst into laughter and I didn't want him to see me. This made me realize that I should look around before I shout out again because "They" may take me away—and you know what a short trip that is.

180

Creating Inner Cheerleaders

Many of us have spent a lifetime trying to identify who or what has stood in the way of our happiness or success. I wrote in the beginning of this book about how some of our Committee members have sabotaged our ability to exalt in who and what we are. However, it is important to acknowledge those people who were there for us or, at the very least, to choose or create someone who becomes our resident cheerleader.

My grandmother Francesca, my grandfather Lorenzo, and my mother are all part of my

cheerleader network. Whenever I feel undernur-
tured, I hear my grandmother's voice telling me
not to worry. "I make you a few little meatballs,
you'll feel fine." These memories sustain and nourish me. My grandfather's big booming voice round-
ing up the family for spaghetti feasts reminds me
of the many wonderful meals and conversations
we had, and my mother's constant reminder that
"You can do it" helps me complete many a project. My family, my dear friends, and my spiritual
beliefs get me through some of my dark times.

Comic Asides

Have you ever been in a situation where you've
become a broken record and no one hears you
anymore? Your level of frustration is at an all-time
high, and you're at your wit's end. Don't give up;
instead, try a little theatrical ploy. Let's face it, we
all get dramatic, but we keep doing reruns of *Friday
the 13th* instead of *Mrs. Doubtfire.*

If you've asked your husband to pick up his
underwear and put it in the hamper for the thou-
sandth time and you keep getting that preopera-
tive drug-induced stare, try a little comic aside.
Naturally, for this to be effective, he has to be present. Say what you normally say, but then answer
yourself back. For example: "Well, look at this, it's
the underwear again. Can you imagine, Jack, it's
all over the place! Do me a favor, will you? Pick

it up and put it in the hamper." Now answer for your husband, but in the way you'd like to hear it: "Sure, hon, I can't wait. I'll do it right away. Anything to make you happy, honey. I'm starving, but I can put that on hold, just for you." Try it with your kids: "Johnny, will you take out the trash?" Answer back: "Oh, I'd love to, Mom. I can't tell you how much I love to take out trash, more than listening to Smashing Pumpkins, more than life itself."

Try it at work: "Well, time to fill up the coffeepot again, so I don't get dregs from the bottom." Answer: "Not a problem, I always do it, so why not continue?" You can add a second character who responds to what you're saying and goes along with you. You can even create a whole cast of characters. Your friends and family might think you've gone off the deep end, but who cares? You were already drowning. This gives you a chance to float.

Ta-Dah Number Ten:
Tolerate More, and Give Thanks Often

Often we're rushing about so much that we become incredibly intolerant of others. One way to relieve stress in our modern-day world is a very simple one: Take the time for manners. When I was a little girl, my grandmother spent hours teaching me manners. "Don't chew with your mouth open," "Put your fork down when you're not eating," "Think before you speak," "Don't mumble." These instructions, plus many more, had a dual purpose: They helped me function better in society, and they were a source of pride for Francesca. To my grandmother, there was no greater sin than being ill-mannered. It brought disgrace upon her good name. For that she reserved the ultimate punishment—silence.

Silence from an elderly Sicilian grandmother can be compared to life imprisonment. An entire act accompanied the silence—great sighs, heavy walking while rosary beads were set to clanking furiously, and hand gestures similar to what the Roman emperors gave to those who were about to die. This would go on for what seemed like forever. Finally my grandfather Lorenzo would come to my rescue and yell "*Basta!*" (Enough!) in his umpire's voice. He was the only one, aside from God, who had the power to end the punishment.

183

Why did manners go away? Part of the reason is that mothers, grandmothers, and whole families have less contact with each other because everyone is working. Another reason is because much of our communication is conducted through equipment—computers, faxes, telephones—rather than face to face. There seems to be little time for the amenities of the past, let alone an acknowledgment of someone else's need for polite treatment.

One of the most ill-mannered aspects of modern life is what I call *appointment interruptus*—being constantly interrupted by telephone calls and/or questions from secretaries, children, and the like, while having an appointment with a business associate or friend. I find this situation particularly irritating if I'm paying for it.

An appointment is a period of time set aside for the individual who made the appointment. Emergencies aside, everyone else should wait until you are done. If it's that important, they should make an appointment. Trying to have a conversation and being told to "Wait a minute while I take this call" is maddening. They might as well say, "I'm sorry, but you're not as important as the person who's calling." Wouldn't it be exciting to know that all calls were being held and no one could barge in until you were done? Think how much faster the appointment would end!

184

Manners also have been undermined by one of technology's horrid little gifts—call waiting or, more to the point, call rude. As you speak, you hear a click and the person you're talking to says, "Hold on, I've got someone else on the line." You're left in the void while the other caller is attended to. I have dangled for as long as five minutes. Can you imagine if people acted like this while you were waiting for service at a department store? "Excuse me, someone has come in behind you and I'll wait on them now. I'll be back to you soon." Riots would ensue!

Human survival is dependent on healthy relating. The complex, ongoing process of people interacting requires understanding, kindness, consideration, and acknowledgment—which is what manners are all about. Having good manners can be a pleasure in itself. It's hard to worry when you're taking the time to be polite, tolerant, and considerate of other people. The poet William Blake sums it up beautifully: "Everything that lives, Lives not alone, Nor for itself."

Hand in hand with being more tolerant and mannerly comes giving thanks more often. Thank that bank teller when she gives you your receipt. Thank your co-worker for filling the Xerox machine with paper when it ran out. Thank the grocery clerk for bagging your groceries. Thank your children for cleaning up without your having to remind them. Thank your husband for taking the kids to the park on Sunday so you could go for your jog. Thank your wife for calling your mother every day when she was sick.

185

You can thank the universe/God/the creator, too. Thank the universe for giving you life. Give thanks for your health and mental well-being. Appreciate the beauty of nature and of sunsets. Thank your God. Say grace before a meal. These expressions of gratitude will make you realize that, actually, you are very lucky. And that's a good thing to know.

๑๑ ๑๑ ๑๑   ๑๑ ๑๑ ๑๑

CHAPTER 11

LORETTA'S JOY JOURNAL

Joy is the inner song you play throughout your day. Joy is an attitude; it comes from a sense of love for yourself and others. It comes from inner peace, the capacity to give and receive, and the ability to appreciate. It is a feeling of gratitude for the gift of life.

In this chapter, you're going to focus on things that you're grateful for in your life. We need to recognize the things we have versus the things we think we need. Keeping a joy journal will help you maintain a feeling of elation—the sense that you're soaring with the eagles instead of scratching in the dirt with the turkeys.

Keep your own joy journal on a blank pad of paper or use a notebook.

1. Before you go to sleep, write down three kind things that were done for you today. Now write down three things you did for someone else. Remember that kindnesses come with no strings. They are done, then let go of.

2. Think of a person or persons who have really made a difference in your life.

3. Think of a way you could surprise and delight someone you love tomorrow.

4. List at least four things that you do well.

5. Write down ten things that you like about yourself.

6. Think of a time when you had so much love in your heart, you could have burst. Write it down.

7. Think of your favorite physical activities as a child (biking, swimming, skipping rope). List them, and make plans to do them again.

8. Write down three things that your children have done well lately. Comment on this out loud, preferably in the presence of others.

9. Think of five qualities that you adore in your partner or spouse. Write them down, and tell your significant other about them.

10. Think of three authors, artists, or musicians who've inspired you or whose work you've simply enjoyed. Make a promise to yourself that you'll read, view, or listen to their work again soon.

11. Remember a time when you felt supported and nurtured in an hour of need. Describe this time and how you felt.

12. Remember three times when you felt inner peace and serenity. As you recapture the feeling, write it down.

13. What obstacles have you overcome recently? Thank yourself and whoever helped you.

14. Think of someone you might forgive and how that might change your life.

15. What is your favorite food? What kinds of sensations do you get when you think of it?

16. Whom do you laugh with the most? Remember a time you laughed so hard, you thought you'd collapse.

17. Remember a wonderful place you've been to and how it made you feel.

18. What song or songs make your heart sing?

19. What is your favorite thing to do? How does it make you feel?

190

20. What is your greatest source of pleasure, and why?

21. When you're in nature, what attracts you the most (plants, animals, trees, mountains, oceans, lakes, etc.)?

22. If you were to leave this planet tomorrow, what would you want people to remember about you?

23. Can you think of one quality that you'd like to work on that could increase your potential for joy (for instance, patience, compassion, kindness, empathy, encouragement)?

24. Is there someone you know who could profit from your understanding and love, and who might need it today?

25. Write down a list of things you're thankful for. Add to it every day. Share the list with others.

Now that you're on your way to a more positive outlook, don't forget one important thing: In order to love others, you have to love yourself. Practice saying "I love you" to yourself in the mirror. Say it with real meaning. Look at yourself and smile. Smile at the wrinkles and crow's-feet. You earned those lines.

Now go out and say "I love you" to the important people in your life. It may be hard to get the words out at first, but it will get easier and easier the more you practice.

And remember, if you laugh, the whole world will laugh with you. Try to keep some humor in your life, even in the hard times. It will help you get through difficulties and will lighten your days. No one ever said on his or her deathbed, "I wish I hadn't laughed so much."

֍ ֍ ֍   ֍ ֍ ֍

RESOURCES FOR HEALTH, HEALING, AND HUMOR

Authentic Happiness: Using the New Positive Psychology to Realize Your Potential for Lasting Fulfillment, by Martin E.P. Seligman. Free Press, 2004.

The Big Book of Stress Relief Games: Quick, Fun Activities for Feeling Better, by Robert Epstein. McGraw-Hill, 2000.

Business Stress Relief: Practical Advice: How to Use Humor to Reduce Stress and Improve Results, by Howard Reiss. AuthorHouse, 2004.

The Complete Idiot's Guide to Beating Stress, by Arlene Matthews Uhl. Alpha Books, 2006.

The Cortisol Connection: Why Stress Makes You Fat and Ruins Your Health—and What You Can Do About It, by Shawn M. Talbott and William Kraemer. Hunter House, 2002.

The End of Stress as We Know It, by Bruce S. McEwen and Elizabeth Norton Lasley. Dana Press, 2004.

50 Ways to Prevent and Manage Stress, by M. Sara Rosenthal. McGraw-Hill, 2001.

Half Empty, Half Full: Understanding the Psychological Roots of Optimism, by Susan C. Vaughan. Harvest Books, 2001.

Hot Stones and Funny Bones: Teens Helping Teens Cope with Stress and Anger, by Brian Seaward and Linda Bartlett. HCI Teens, 2002.

Learned Optimism: How to Change Your Mind and Your Life, by Martin E.P. Seligman. Vintage, 2006.

The Little Book Of Stress, by Rohan Candappa. Andrews McMeel Publishing, 2000.

194

POWER Optimism: Enjoy the Life You Have . . . Create the Success You Want, by Dana Lightman. POWER Optimism, LLC, 2004.

The Relaxation & Stress Reduction Workbook, by Martha Davis, Matthew McKay, and Elizabeth Robbins Eshelman. New Harbinger Publications, 2000.

SOS: A Girl's Guide to Sex, Optimism, and Surviving the 21st Century, by Helen Hawkes. Kensington, 2004.

Stress Can Really Get on Your Nerves! by Trevor Romain and Elizabeth Verdick. Free Spirit Publishing, 2000.

The Stress Cure: A Simple, 7-Step Plan to Help Women Balance Mood, Improve Memory, and Restore Energy, by Dr. Vern Cherewatenko and Paul Perry. HarperCollins, 2004.

Stress-Free Performance Appraisals: Turn Your Most Painful Management Duty into a Powerful Motivational Tool, by Sharon Armstrong and Madelyn Appelbaum. Career Press, 2003.

Stress Survival Guide: An Essential Guide to Coping with the Pressures of Everyday Life, by Jit Gill. HarperTorch, 2003.

25 Natural Ways to Manage Stress and Avoid Burnout: A Mind-Body Approach to Well-Being, by James Scala. McGraw-Hill, 2000.

You Can't Be Serious! Putting Humor to Work, by Michael Kerr. Michael Kerr, 2001.

ᏮᎧ ᏮᎧ ᏮᎧ   ᏮᎧ ᏮᎧ ᏮᎧ

ORGANIZATIONS

Association for Applied and Therapeutic Humor (AATH)
http://www.aath.org

The Humor Project
480 Broadway, Suite 210
Saratoga Springs, NY 12866
(518) 587-8770
http://www.humorproject.com

The International Society for Humor Studies (ISHS)
http://www.hnu.edu/ishs/

World Humor Organization
Chicken Lips Comedy Theater
http://www.chickenlips.com/

☙☙☙　☙☙☙

ACKNOWLEDGMENTS

Thank you to all those who have contributed to making my life and work successful, happy, and fulfilling.

ABOUT THE AUTHOR

Loretta LaRoche, the best-selling author of *Life Is Short—Wear Your Party Pants* and *Squeeze the Day,* among other works, is an internationally renowned stress-management consultant who advocates humor, optimism, and resiliency as coping mechanisms. She uses her wit and wisdom to help people learn how to take stress and turn it into strength, and how to see themselves as the survivors of their own lives—that is, to find the "bless in the mess."

Loretta is a favorite with viewers of her six PBS specials, as well as on the lecture circuit, where she presents an average of 100 talks per year. She lives in Plymouth, Massachusetts.

Website: **www.LorettaLaroche.com**

☜☞ ☜☞ ☜☞   ☜☞ ☜☞ ☜☞

NOTES

NOTES

NOTES

NOTES

NOTES

NOTES

NOTES

NOTES

NOTES

NOTES